The Silent Shackle

Captives of the Crescent

by

Dr. ant

The Silent Shackle: Captives of the Crescent

Contents

Introduction

Chapter 1: The Historical Context of Caucasian Slavery

Origins of Slavery in the Ottoman Empire
Comparison with the Transatlantic Slave Trade

Chapter 2: Capture and Transport

The Involvement of Barbary Pirates
Raid Strategies and Targeted Regions

Chapter 3: Life as a Slave in the Ottoman Empire

Daily Struggles and Labor
Inhumane Treatment and Punishments

Chapter 4: The Economic Impact of Slavery on the Ottoman Empire

Revenue from Slave Markets
Economic Dependencies and Growth

Chapter 5: The Social Hierarchy and Roles of Slaves

Integration into Ottoman Society
Resistance and Rebellion

Chapter 6: European Reactions and Responses

Diplomatic Efforts to End Slavery
Public Perception and Media Coverage

Chapter 7: The Legacy of Caucasian Slavery

Long-Term Effects on Europe and the Ottoman Empire
Modern Historical Narratives

Chapter 8: Comparison with African Slavery

Key Differences in Treatment and Labor
Statistical Comparisons

Chapter 9: Contemporary Discourse on Slavery

Modern Ignorance and Apathy
Historical Revisionism and Its Consequences

Chapter 10: Addressing Historical Injustices

Reparative Measures and Memorials
Healing and Moving Forward

Chapter 11: The Role of Historians in Shaping Memory

Investigating and Spreading Awareness
Advocacy and Public Engagement

Chapter 12: Bridging Divides in Modern Society

Lessons from History for Today's Issues
Forging a Path Toward Unity

Conclusion

Appendix A: Appendix

Introduction

Amidst the cold and somber corridors of history, there lies a story seldom illuminated by the meager flickers of scholarly inquiry. This narrative, imbued with the lingering chill of past tragedies, winds through the epochs, revealing the plight of Caucasian slaves within the labyrinthine shadows of the Ottoman Empire. The genesis of this seldom-discussed enslavement intertwines with threads of piracy, economic exploitation, and a bewildering social hierarchy, each contributing to the mosaic of suffering and resilience that dawns upon our modern understanding.

Echoing through the annals of time, the specter of Caucasian slavery bespeaks a reality steeped in both darkness and relentless human endeavor. Were it not for the barbary pirates, fierce as the stormy rage of Poseidon, who cast their nets over the Mediterranean and beyond, reeling in souls to be traded as mere goods, the empire's vast tapestry of human bondage might have been very different. The marbled halls and grand bazaars of the Ottoman realm bore silent witness to the torment endured by countless lives, souls disparate and distant from their homelands.

In traversing the dim-lit corridors of such a grave history, one cannot remain indifferent to the myriad intricacies and haunting nocturnes that define this epoch. The harrowing journeys across tempestuous seas, the brutal conditions aboard the ill-fated vessels, and the inhumane punishments typify an existence reduced to sheer endurance. In these reflections, a gloomy chiaroscuro reveals not just the undercurrents of pain but also the flickers of defiance, of slaves who dared to resist, to reclaim fragments of their humanity amidst the profane degradations.

Understand, then, revered scholars, that our pursuit is not merely one of recounting tales from the misty past but of peeling back the layers of ornate manipulations that have often sanitized or altogether ignored these harrowing truths. The legacies of Caucasian enslavement extend their spectral hands into contemporary times, shaping societal perceptions and informing modern struggles albeit in often overlooked corners of academic and public consciousness. As we unearth these chapters buried in the dust of oblivion, our endeavor carries the gravitas of righting historical wrongs and addressing troubling inaccuracies that pervade the modern discourse of slavery.

It is within this academic crucible that we must address a grim reality: the institutionalized ignorance and apathy that shroud the subject of Caucasian slavery. As the vestiges of this cruel epoch linger in the subconscious fabric of contemporary society, our scholarly pursuits become both a lantern of knowledge and a weapon against historical myopia. The task, therefore, compels us to delve with meticulous zeal into the records, the ruins, and the relics, illuminating the obscure corners where the light of critical scrutiny has seldom reached.

The pursuit of understanding this troubled chapter cries out for a comprehensive examination—a juxtaposition against the more widely acknowledged transatlantic slave trade, a probe into the economic forces at play, and an exploration of the social hierarchies that dictated the fates of countless individuals. For within this harsh tableau lay the seeds of intricate economic dependencies, where the sinews of human labor intertwined with the financial growth and stratified societal structures of the Ottoman power.

However, to merely recount the cruelties inflicted upon these souls would be a gross injustice to their memory. Woven through the dark tapestry are stories of formidable resilience, of quiet acts of rebellion, and of an enduring human spirit that defied the chains of their captors. Each narrative fork adds a layer of complexity to our understanding, urging us to transcend simplistic historical binaries and embrace a nuanced discourse that acknowledges both suffering and resistance, degradation and courage.

Thus, we embark upon this solemn exploration not as mere chroniclers of woe but as harbingers of a more profound understanding, one that seeks to rectify historical oversights and to bridge the divides wrought by an incomplete historical narrative. Addressing the injustices imposed upon Caucasian slaves requires an interdisciplinary approach that leverages historical narratives, economic analysis, and the power of public memory.

If history is indeed a mirror, then let it be an undistorted one—reflecting both the darkness and the latent quest for justice clouded within its grim visages.

In examining the repercussions of this overlooked epoch, one must consider not only the immediate impacts but the enduring legacy that has shaped the cultural and social mores of subsequent generations. The residues of this past emerge in subtle yet profound ways across modern Europe and the once-sprawling Ottoman territories. As we discern these intricate patterns, the contemporary historian's role becomes ever more vital, entwined with both academic rigor and a moral responsibility to advocate for a more equitable reconstruction of our shared past.

Historical revisionism and its consequences loom large in this context. The oft-marginalized narratives cry for an ethical reading, an earnest scholarly engagement that transcends mere documentation to foster genuine understanding and reconciliation. Herein lies the crux of our scholarly quest: to navigate the tempestuous waters of historical discourse with both a discerning eye and a compassionate heart, carving out spaces for the silenced voices that echo through time.

The present endeavor, therefore, serves a dual purpose: to illuminate the myriad dimensions of Caucasian slavery and to employ these historical insights in addressing pressing contemporary social issues. Expounding upon these hidden recesses of our shared past not only enriches our historical fabric but impels us towards a future that acknowledges and learns from these grievous chapters.

Through the subsequent chapters, we shall unveil the darkened folds of history with an unwavering commitment to academic precision and ethical clarity. We shall navigate the intricate interplay of economic, social, and political forces that shaped the lived experiences of Caucasian slaves. We will contrast these findings with the broader canvas of human bondage, especially through the comparative lens of African slavery, to extract nuanced understandings and potent learnings for our current societal dilemmas.

As we unmask the harrowing yet essential stories submerged in the obscure depths of the Ottoman past, let us remain mindful of the transformative power of historical inquiry. The narrative woven here is not solely one of desolation but one imbued with the resilience of the human spirit—an homage and a call to acknowledge, rectify, and ultimately heal the fractures borne of forgotten injustices.

Welcome, then, valiant scholars, to this dark and profound journey through the annals of forgotten histories. May this exploration serve as both a beacon and a bulwark against the tides of ignorance, igniting a fervent pursuit of truth and justice in our academic and social realms.

Chapter 1: The Historical Context of Caucasian Slavery

In the cobwebbed corridors of antiquity, where twilight shadows the annals of forgotten histories, one finds the eerie specter of Caucasian slavery. Here, in the tormented embrace of yesteryears, the Ottoman Empire emerges as a ravenous beast, its talons sinking deep into the flesh of myriad souls. Charted waters teem with the clamor of Barbary pirates, their sinister whispers filling the sails of ships bound for lands unforgiving and desolate. This somber tableau, akin to a tragic play where every actor knows their dreadful fate, unfolds against the menacing backdrop of imperial ambitions and nightmares born from human greed. This malevolent tide washed through Europe, setting a precedent only to be rivaled by the harrowing saga of the Transatlantic slave trade. Observe, then, as we delve into this dark chapter of human bondage, where the unholy marriage of commerce and cruelty birthed a legacy stained in blood and sorrow, casting an interminable shadow over the subsequent epochs.

Origins of Slavery in the Ottoman Empire

The genesis of slavery within the expanse of the Ottoman Empire is enshrouded in the mists of time, a harrowing tale of human suffering that wove itself into the very fabric of an empire. From the jagged peaks of the Caucasus Mountains, myriad souls were torn from their homes, ensnared by the relentless gears of avarice and conflict. These captives, bound and betrayed, were thrust into a whirlwind of subjugation that saw their identities stripped and their fates sealed. Within the labyrinthine corridors of power, the Ottoman elite, driven by an insatiable thirst for dominion and economic enrichment, turned the machinery of slavery into a finely-tuned instrument of statecraft and wealth. The institutions of the empire, cloaked in a facade of magnificence and order, masked the profound suffering of these Caucasian captives whose lives became mere commodities in a vast and heartless trade. As the tides of history surged and receded, these chains of bondage laid the grim foundations upon which the empire's grandeur stood.

The Role of Barbary Pirates in Slave Trade …In this grim tableau of history, the Barbary Pirates emerge like specters from the dark recesses of human cruelty, casting long shadows over the Mediterranean's azure waters. These fearsome marauders, operating primarily out of North African strongholds such as Algiers, Tunis, and Tripoli, were not merely plunderers; they were meticulous architects of despair, deeply enmeshed in the macabre commerce of human lives. Their activities are marred by the contrivance of systemic terror and exploitation, preying upon the vulnerabilities of coastal European communities.

The modus operandi of Barbary Pirates was as calculating as it was brutal. They would launch nocturnal raids on unsuspecting European villages, leaving a trail of destruction in their wake. Entire populations were often dragged from their beds, shackled, and herded onto waiting corsair ships. These captives were then transported across the Mediterranean, their fates sealed as they entered the bustling and ruthless slave markets of the Ottoman Empire. The human cargo was not random; strategic acumen guided the selection of victims. Artisans, sailors, and young women were among the most coveted, fetching higher prices and thus maximizing the pirates' profits.

The very mention of Barbary pirates summoned dread across coastal Europe. For centuries, fishermen, merchants, and villagers alike lived in the shadow of these marauders. The pirates weren't bound by the rules of conventional warfare; their style was guerrilla, their appearance sudden, and their impact devastating. The impact they had on European society was profound, instilling a collective trauma that simmered in the corridors of historical memory. Families were torn apart overnight, husbands separated from wives, and children from parents, each journeying into a dark unknown.

It was not merely greed that drove the Barbary Pirates but also a complex web of geopolitical stratagem. Algiers, Tunis, and Tripoli benefited from the Ottoman aegis that provided implicit if not explicit support. These pirates acted as rogue agents, an outlier force that expanded the Ottoman influence through maritime terror. The bustling slave markets of Algiers and Istanbul could be viewed as microcosms of human despair, the lifeblood of empires flourishing on the anguish of coerced labor.

It is essential to note that the enslaved individuals were not solely fated to laborious toils but also to be pawns in a game of diplomatic chess. Christendom in Europe and Ottoman hegemony found an almost perverse form of communication through the medium of captured souls. Ransoms would be negotiated, treaties brokered, each life a bargaining chip in larger geopolitical negotiations. This turned slaves into a form of currency, their value fluctuating with the tides of political expediency.

The routes plied by these vessels of despair often form a macabre tapestry of suffering. From the Italian coastlines to the distant shores of Iceland, few regions were spared the reach of Barbary Pirates' long arms. The infamous "Sack of Baltimore" in Ireland in 1631 stands as a stark reminder of their far-reaching grip. Dozens were seized, shipped away, and never seen again. The everyday labor, the familial ties, all shattered like fragile glass upon the anvils of these pirates' relentless ambitions.

The inner workings of slave auctions contribute yet more layers to this history of woe. Upon reaching the Ottoman slave markets, captives were stripped of whatever remained of their former identities. Documents and personal belongings were burned or discarded, ensuring that those shackled would fade into anonymity. The marketplace echoed with frantic bidding, the bleating of livestock intermingling with the cries of despairing souls. A young woman, her value appraised through a ghoulish combination of age, beauty, and potential reproductive capabilities, might find herself wrenched into harem life. Artisans and sailors were often destined for grueling work, their skills turned against them in twisted irony.

For historians, the archival remnants that document these dark chapters are filled with harrowing testimonies and chilling accounts. Diaries, official records, and ecclesiastic correspondences paint a vivid yet somber picture. In the remarkable narrative of Thomas Pellow, an Englishman captured and enslaved for over two decades, the realities of life under Barbary Pirate captivity are illuminated with raw authenticity. Pellow, captured at age eleven, recounts endless hours of labor, meticulous indoctrination into Islam, and frequent episodes of torment, all underscored by a yearning for freedom that never waned.

European powers were not merely passive victims in this grim tale but were often complicit in the systemic failure to thwart these raids. The reluctance or inability to protect coastal settlements highlights their strategic precariousness and political distractions elsewhere. Attempts at military responses and naval engagements bore mixed results, often stymied by the adeptness and cunning of pirate tactics. The Treaty of Peace and Commerce between England and Algiers in 1662, for example, offers a glimpse into the desperate yet pragmatic diplomacy Europe engaged with to stem the tide of piracy. Yet, the tranquility was transient, and any lapse in vigilance was swiftly punished by renewed raids and abductions.

The melancholy refrain of this age-old strife lingered well into the 19th century, dwindling only with increased European naval presence and the eventual decline of Ottoman sea power. By then, countless lives had been altered forever, entire communities shattered, and a palpable sense of vulnerability rooted deep within the European psyche.

In unraveling the tapestry of Barbary Pirates' role in the slave trade, one confronts the multifaceted complexities of human savagery, resilience, and the inexorable pursuit of power. The black sails of their ships no longer haunt the Mediterranean, but the echoes of their deeds reverberate through corridors of history, a perpetual memorial to human suffering and the pernicious capacities of unrestrained avarice and cruelty.

Comparison with the Transatlantic Slave Trade

The annals of history are often bathed in blood and shackled in chains, yet each epoch possesses its unique horrors and tribulations. To draw parallels between Caucasian slavery within the Ottoman Empire and the Transatlantic Slave Trade is to juxtapose distinct realms of cruelty, each bound by its own historical sinews.

The Transatlantic Slave Trade, spanning centuries and continents, harrowingly displaced millions of African souls to the New World. Here, the chattel were subjected to a brutal existence primarily on plantations across the Americas, feeding a voracious economic machine. Conversely, Caucasian slavery—though lesser-known—flourished within the Ottoman dominion, ensnaring primarily inhabitants of Eastern Europe and the Caucasus.

In both systems, the captors endeavored to erase identities and forge laborers from the raw material of human suffering. Yet it was in their methodologies that their paths diverged. The Ottoman slave trade often centered on abducting those of Slavic, Circassian, and Georgian lineage. Kidnapped by Barbary pirates or conscripted through warfare and raids, these captives journeyed under the oppression of crescent moons rather than the unforgiving sun that oversaw the Middle Passage.

Transport of slaves across the Atlantic painted the dark sea with an indelible stain. Packed like sardines aboard dilapidated ships, the African captives faced extreme dehumanization, disease, and mortality. By contrast, the voyage to the Ottoman realms, though fraught with peril and misery, often placed the enslaved within the vessels of more traditional piracy—where profit was the primary motivation rather than sheer numerical transference of human cargo. The sin remains but yields different shades.

Upon arrival, the abodes of enslavement further delineated the sufferings. In the New World plantations, chains clinked with the rhythm of agriculture and mining, garnering wealth that propelled empires.

Conversely, within the Ottoman Empire, the labor was diversified: some toiled in fields, others served in domestic settings, regiments, or administration. Such dispersion did not dilute the cruelty but merely reorganized it.

Consider the harem and janissary systems. Toto cælo, these represent a distinct feature where the Ottoman practice diverged sharply from the Transatlantic paradigm. In harems, enslaved women from Eastern Europe were transformed into concubines, their bodies becoming instruments of pleasure and political alliance. Male slaves, particularly through the devşirme system, were converted into elite soldiers, the Janissaries—a twisted form of social mobility carved through relentless training and severance from their origins. The Transatlantic trade had no such institutional avenues.

Yet, the economic incentives paralleled. Europe's thirst for sugar, tobacco, and cotton found its macabre satisfaction through African enslavement. Ottoman preferences—whether for soldiers, labor, or domestic servants—spurred on the incessant raids orchestrated by Barbary corsairs and Ottoman expansionism. Thus, monetary gain flowed through rivers of exploitation, irrigating both systems.

The resistance among these enslaved populations also beckons a somber reflection. While slave revolts peppered the annals of both systems, the Transatlantic arena witnessed organized and large-scale rebellions—from Haiti's flames of insurrection to the mutinies aboard slaver ships. Ottoman slaves shared in this spirit of defiance; however, the dispersed nature meant smaller, fragmented uprisings, often stifled within households or squelched by the swift might of local enforcement.

Human suffering in these two spheres also reverberates differently through modern consciousness. The Transatlantic Slave Trade, more pervasive in contemporary narratives, garners broad academic scrutiny and public acknowledgment. Museums, reparative dialogues, and educational frameworks are devoted to its perpetual remembrance. Caucasian slavery within the Ottoman context, shrouded by the mists of historical omission, struggles for similar recognition.

Let us not be enshrouded by the illusion that capturing, trafficking, and enslaving Eastern Europeans involved any measure of leniency. They were forcibly torn from their homes, subjected to violence, forced conversions, and insurmountable hardships. Nevertheless, effective mechanisms for their systemic extermination, which characterized the Transatlantic transport, were largely absent, casting different yet equally tormenting scars upon the historical landscape.

Modern scholars and historians bear the responsibility of excavating these veiled narratives. While the plight of millions transported via the Middle Passage remains a seminal study in human barbarity, the beams of academic inquiry must illuminate the equally tragic spheres of Ottoman Caucasian slavery. Comparative analytics serve as a beacon, revealing the multilayered human costs spanning different epochs.

If we are to forge a bridge of historical understanding, it becomes imperative to engage in a balanced study—neither elevating one martyrdom over another nor diminishing their unique torments. This dual recognition ensures a comprehensive portrayal of humanity's chronic inhumanity, fostering a deeper acknowledgment of our collective past.

The enervation and desolation of Caucasian and African victims are hallmarks of a world that, through bloodlust and avarice, repeatedly turned men and women into mere commodities. The crossroad of comparison lies not in ranking sufferings but in appreciating their singular and combined legacies. The ink of history is enriched by both narratives, urging us toward an unfaltering commitment to justice and memory.

Chapter 2: Capture and Transport

When the Barbary pirates embarked upon their dread endeavors, they cast a veil of dread upon the shores of Europe, particularly targeting the sunlit coasts of Italy, Spain, and France. Their nimble ships, swift as phantoms under moonlight, bore the enslaved from hearth and homeland to the belly of doom. The shackled souls endured the cruel and turbulent seas, captivation wrapped in the echoing travail of despair. Chains became their new garments, and the brine of the ocean mingled with their tears. These voyages were cauldrons of misery, where the stench of death was a constant companion, and hope a rare fugitive. Overcrowded holds reeked with the malady of hopeless laborers, their fate sealed by the iron will of their captors. Each wave that rocked the vessel echoed the tumultuous journey of those condemned, a grim testament to humanity's unyielding cruelty.

The Involvement of Barbary Pirates

Emerging from the veiled shadows of the Mediterranean's perilous coasts, the Barbary pirates were malevolent specters haunting the shores and maritime paths. Renowned for their ruthless precision, they orchestrated raids with chilling efficiency, targeting unsuspecting coastal villages and vessels drifting under the starlit skies. Their marauding endeavors ensnared countless souls, spiriting them away to the grim markets of the Ottoman Empire. These corsairs, driven by both avarice and a zeal for dominance, disrupted the tranquility of European seafarers and settlers alike, transforming serene landscapes into nightmarish vistas of smoke and despair. The captured, wrenched from their homelands, were shackled and thrust into the abyss of human bondage, their fates sealed by the iron fists of their captors. In the throes of capture and transport, agony and dread became their constant companions, echoing through the annals of history as a testament to human cruelty and resilience.

The Conditions on Slave Ships aboard which unfortunate souls faced inhospitable conditions that defy human dignity were a realm of such despair and anguish that words might shudder before daring to describe it. Cramped beneath low wooden decks, the imprisoned felt the oppressive weight of despair. Each inch of space was laden with the suffering of those shackled near their brethren in fate, their breaths barely punctuating the dense, fetid air.

The stench of human excretion intermingled with the acrid odor of saltwater and sweat. The sea's merciless rhythms jolted bodies against one another, straight into splinters of wood and rusted shackles. Rations were meager—hardtack moldy from the sea air, water fouled by weeks of storage. In such conditions, disease ran rampant; fevers burned and infections festered, claiming more lives than the waves themselves.

Beneath the stars, overseers with whips and shouts rendered quarter to no soul. The once-free men and women, now reduced to property, were given no semblance of respect. The shipmaster's ledger reflected cold precision, wherein each human was accounted as mere commodity. The grim tally of mortality was high, yet it altered not the master's cruel calculations; replacements were far too easily obtained from the shorelines continually raided by pirates.

Within this hellish environment, the hierarchy of suffering placed the weakest in the most dire situations. Elders, women, and children bore the cruel mockery of existence, their frames unable to withstand the ruthless toll of maritime transport. Young children often succumbed, their agonized cries swiftly muted by death. Among adults, survival was a matter of grim endurance, their spirits often broken long before their bodies ceased.

At times, daylight filtered through cracks in the ship's wooden hull, casting pale, ghostly shafts of light onto faces etched with misery. The monotony of suffering spanned unbroken days and endless nights, punctuated by sirens of screams during fits of illness or madness. On stormy nights, terror amplified; the ship's violent lurching instilled primal fear of drowning. Cries of the despondent rose louder than the thunder, yet such was their fate, unheard and unanswered.

Yet, in this purgatory, a modicum of resilience could often be discerned; whispered prayers and defiant glimmers in weary eyes held fast against complete despair. Remnants of past identities clung stubbornly within the soul's deepest recesses, a testament to the human spirit enduring beyond breach and bondage. Stark camaraderies formed amidst shared torment, their whispers of home offering ephemeral succor, though they were but specters of solace.

Manacles bit deeply into wrists and ankles, engraining scars that no liberation could ever efface. The physical restrictions mirrored the existential shackles binding their fates. Deprivation and despair hollowed out the strongest among them; however, a stark will to survive often seared brightly against the encroaching darkness. Each day was an ordeal, each hour infused with an ache for lost freedom.

Above deck, the overseers maintained vigilance, ever watchful against insurrections that might brew amidst such desperation. The hierarchy of command was based on terror and brutality; any sign of dissent was quashed immediately, often with lethal force. Chains clinked distrustfully as the enslaved were herded up for brief moments of open air, their bodies grim placeholders in a voyage that promised little more than another prison upon reaching its end.

Slumber, if it came at all, brought neither rest nor reprieve, for nightmares inhabited the fragmented dreams of captives. Visions of lost families, forsaken homes, and the violence of their capture haunted every sleeping breath. Even the restless waves themselves seemed to taunt with the memory of freedom, whispering cruel reminders through the wooden confines.

Shipboard politics played a grim tune as captains and procurers negotiated their human cargo's worth upon docking. These discussions sealed the grim travesties yet to manifest in the lives of those who would be auctioned off as livestock. Each slaver's fortuity was built upon the broken backs of countless men, women, and children, their sorrow transmuted into mercantile value, devoid of humanity's light.

The dread journey often spanned weeks, each day a monotonous tapestry of hunger, torment, and despair. Beneath decks, the bonds of physical and psychological fetters endured, bending but rarely breaking under the dire strain of inhumanity. The belly of the ship bore witness to the most profound depths of human wretchedness, each plank and beam imbued with the cries and tears of generations thrust into unfathomable suffering.

Naught but the vast ocean horizon and the relentless toll of time marked the passage of this infernal voyage. As the land hove into view, the enslaved might clutch embers of hope, though it was often nothing but a cruel lie. Docking marked merely the transition from one form of imprisonment to another, new enslavement concealed within the guise of bustling markets and public auctions.

The reflective nature of this solemn chapter reminds us, dear comrades in history, of the immense weight each person bore, each life altered irreparably. Their stories, etched in the annals of such a horrific practice, prompt us to understand the full measure of suffering faced on those cursed vessels. Unfathomable grief and unyielding endurance pervade this legacy, impelling future generations to recount, to remember, and, one hopes, never to repeat.

Raid Strategies and Targeted Regions

The bleak orchestration of Caucasian slavery began with the meticulously planned raids of Barbary pirates, whose ships loomed as harbingers of doom across the Mediterranean coasts. Fueled by malevolence, greed, and a desire for dominance, these maritime marauders deployed strategies that were both ruthless and cunning. The entrapment of unsuspecting villages often unfolded under the shroud of night, cloaked in malevolence, to exploit the vulnerability of unguarded settlements.

To comprehend the magnitude of these invasions, one must delve into the methodical operations that underpinned the pirates' success. Preparation was key. Surveillance missions, covertly executed by scouts, provided crucial insights about the target's defenses, the number of inhabitants, potential routes of ambush, and the prosperity of the village. Such scrupulous reconnaissance ensured that the pirates struck with surgical precision and maximal impact.

Regions along the European coastline, notably Italy, Spain, and the southern territories of France, presented lucrative targets due to their proximity to North Africa. The western coasts of the Iberian Peninsula, frequented by prosperous maritime traffic, became particularly desirable. Yet, the spoils were not confined to these regions alone. Venturing further into the British Isles, from Cornwall's savage cliffs to Ireland's verdant shores, the pirates expanded their reign of terror. The Norse settlements, basking in a deceptive tranquility, proved an alluring target.

When the pirates descended upon their victims, the initial moments were left to agonizing ambiguity—an eerie prelude to the impending calamity. Unannounced, the raiders would rush ashore, overwhelming the coastal guard or infiltrating through rarely patrolled entry points. They wielded not just weapons but knowledge, exploiting local topographies and disenfranchised populations who, coerced or bribed, provided internal sabotage. The towns, bereft of warning, were left defenceless to the brigades of marauding men.

Understanding their maritime prowess, one must acknowledge the pirates' almost predatory proficiency in employing swift vessels, agile enough to navigate treacherous waters but substantial in their cargo capacity. Galleys propelled by relentless rowers allowed raiders to outmaneuver slower naval patrols, affording them escape before retaliation could be mustered.

The human cost of these raids was staggering. Entire cohorts of villagers, sometimes numbering in the hundreds, were shackled, and herded like cattle to the waiting slave ships, forced onto a maritime journey of unspeakable misery. Families disassembled, and identities obliterated; the emotional toll was cataclysmic. The captives were condemned to lives of overbearing futility, interned in darkness both literal and metaphorical.

The physical logistics of such catastrophic operations necessitated a gruesome efficiency. Collusion with land-based agents, such as the wealthy corsair patrons in Algiers and Tunis, facilitated swift-offs and transitions from maritime confines to inland slave markets. These local patrons knew the terrain, possessed the means to bribe officials and knew precisely how to distribute human chattel to maximize profit. The fate of the captives was often sealed before they even arrived in the bustling slave markets of North Africa.

Despite the nightmarish urgency, the pirates demonstrated a grotesque adherence to order. The intentions were never to simply obliterate. The objective circling like a vulture was the acquisition of labor, leveraging the captured souls into a sprawling system of trade. The methodical inhumanity was strategically calculated to ensure maximum retainment and transport of slaves with minimal loss, a decision driven by the cold calculus of commerce.

Throughout the 16th to the 18th centuries, certain regions fell victim more recurrently than others, resulting in local populations developing rudimentary defensive strategies. Villagers constructed watchtowers and crude fortifications, and village militias formed, trained, and weaponized. Yet, with rare exceptions, these defences proved tragically inadequate against the sophisticated onslaught. When brute force betrayed their enterprises, the pirates resorted to subterfuge, using misinformation to stir confusion or lull the villagers into complacency before striking.

Collateral damage, while not the primary intent, was a frequent by-product of these merciless raids. Houses burned to smouldering ruins, leaving the air thick with acrid sorrow, and echoes of cries and clashing steel reverberated through the desolate coasts. Some chose the tragic solace of the waves, preferring to drown rather than face the shackles of slavery, their final acts of defiance lost to the indifferent sea.

The Ottoman Empire's role in these operations must also be emphasized. Their unofficial endorsement and support of the Barbary raiders were pivotal in sustaining these maritime marauders. The empire's strategic ambitions extended beyond land; dominating maritime trade routes was essential. With a tacit nod from Istanbul, the Barbary pirates became the de facto privateers, hindering European naval expansion and inflicting economic damage through the capture of human and material bounty.

As the raids progressed with dismal regularity, the affected regions experienced demographic shifts and an enduring atmosphere of paranoia. Tales of abduction lingered, becoming part of local folklore, both myth and grim reality. The psychological footprint of these marauding invasions imprinted fear and suspicion onto generations that followed, shaping the cultural narrative for centuries.

In rural settings, the absence of a robust defense framework turned inhabitants into easy targets. Agrarian villages—fertile and bustling in peace—often had no inkling of impending doom until it was too late. Their isolation worked against them, with their cries for help dissolving into the deafening silence of the plains. Coastal communities, whose livelihoods thrived on the sea, ironically found themselves betrayed by the very waters offering sustenance.

With so frequent incursions, an unholy synergy developed between the marauders and local bandits. The pirates' ferocity was matched by inland brigands, who exploited the chaos to plunder and enslave. A chaotic theatre of betrayal, with farmers and fishermen caught in the crossfire, left behind nothing but despair and desolation.

Piratical leaders, notorious for their brutal efficiency, took on near-mythical proportions. The dread invoked by names such as Khayr al-Din

Barbarossa or Murat Reis ensured that even the hint of their presence could cause entire towns to capitulate preemptively. Their reliance on fear and surprise was akin to conducting a macabre symphony of human suffering.

It's imperative to understand the confluence of factors—economic, political, and geographical—that rendered certain regions perennial targets. Wealthier coastal cities often found themselves contrastingly well-prepared, at least diplomatically, with ransoms poised and emissaries dispatched to negotiate for their citizens' release. Meanwhile, poorer and isolated communities became almost resigned to their fate, a haunting acceptance hardened by repeated injustices.

Equipped with the intricate strategies and relentless efficacy of these maritime marauders, history paints a somber portrait of human resilience in the face of almost perennial subjugation.

Chapter 3: Life as a Slave in the Ottoman Empire

In the shadowy corridors of the Ottoman dynasty, lives bent under the harsh yoke of slavery, each breath a silent testament to untold anguish. These souls, severed from their homelands like branches torn from their roots, found themselves ensnared in a world of dread and relentless toil. From the pebbled gardens of opulent estates to the parched expanses of fields under the pitiless sun, every dawn brought with it labor so grueling it scalded the spirit. The torturous lash, the iron chains—emblems of their suffering—served not merely as instruments of punishment but as grim reminders of a life stripped of freedom and dignity. Innocence and faith, crushed beneath the weight of ceaseless expectations, offered little solace. Thus, within these labyrinthine walls and sprawling lands, myriad tales of sorrow unfolded, each more desolate than the last, carving a somber legacy into the annals of Ottoman history.

Daily Struggles and Labor

The daily existence for a slave in the Ottoman Empire was nothing short of a relentless torment. The break of dawn heralded a ceaseless cycle of toil and submission, where their every breath hinged upon the whims of their oppressors. Men, women, and children alike were burdened with grueling tasks, from straining in the expansive fields to slaving away within the confines of grand households. The yoke of labor was harsh and unremitting, leaving them with little respite and less hope. In the fields, they bled under the scorching sun, while in the opulent mansions, their servitude was marked by constant vigilance and the sting of the lash. Such a life was a shadowy existence where dreams of freedom were as distant as a mirage, and the chains of labor were inescapably real.

Work in Fields and Households brought its harrowing intricacies to the very heart of the Caucasian slaves' experience. Each dawn heralded not just a new day, but an unrelenting cycle of labor, stripping these souls of any semblance of freedom. Their daily existence stretched across the verdant expanses and the dimly lit quarters of Ottoman households, ushering in a life defined by toil and torment.

On the sprawling fields, every furrow carved into the earth bore witness to their agony. The sun, a cruel overseer, beat down upon their backs as they worked the land from dawn to dusk. The sheer physicality of the labor was a testament to their endurance—plowing, planting, harvesting—tasks demanding both strength and stoicism. These fields were not just the foundation of agricultural output but also an arena where human endurance was tested to the extreme.

The Ottoman agrarian economy heavily relied on slave labor. Each harvest season, slaves were pushed beyond the brink, under the vigilance of their overseers. Those who faltered faced the sting of whips. The fields became a stage where the human spirit was both crushed and forged. Whispered tales of fleeting rebellions sometimes fluttered through, like ghostly apparitions, only to be violently quenched by the unyielding hand of authority.

Transitioning from the harsh sunlit fields to the subdued interiors of Ottoman households did not signify an escape from hardship. The manor houses of the affluent, with their intricate mosaics and lavish furnishings, were but gilded cages for the unfortunate souls tethered within. Bound to their masters' will, household slaves played roles that spanned the gamut from menial servants to trusted aides.

Within these grand estates, domestic slaves performed myriad duties. From the break of dawn, the rhythmic clatter of utensils and the scent of early morning fires permeated their routine. They scrubbed, washed, and prepared meals under the watchful eyes of their mistresses and masters. Their stations in kitchens, storerooms, and halls interlaced their fates with the very fabric of Ottoman domestic life, yet constantly reaffirmed their subjugation.

Some slaves found themselves entrusted with the care of their masters' offspring. These were delicate bonds fraught with complex emotions. While some forged sincere relationships with the children under their care, many others were reminded daily of their disposability and the fragile veneer of trust placed upon them. They were caregivers by necessity, pouring love into lives that would one day grow into their oppressors.

The dichotomy of work in fields and households exhibited an intricate dance between power and subjugation, an endless interplay of proximity and alienation. The slaves' omnipresence was essential yet methodically compartmentalized to avoid threats to the social hierarchy. Their suffering was perceived not with empathy but as a necessary cog in the grand machinery of the empire.

Be it the cold, impersonal expanse of the farm or the cloistered, intimate spaces of the home, the specter of punishment loomed large. Whips and chains were the tools of enforcement, muting resistance before it could surface. However, resistance was not extinguished entirely. Subtle acts of defiance, minor sabotage, or stolen moments of respite were testaments to a resilient spirit struggling against inexorable odds.

The dichotomy between fieldwork and household duties not only dictated the physical reality for Caucasian slaves but also shaped their psychological landscape. The often brutal, backbreaking labor under the open sky contrasted sharply with the sometimes intricate and mentally taxing tasks within the shelter of walls. The slaves' bodies and minds were tested ceaselessly, their spirits kept in a constant state of weariness by forces both natural and human-made.

Though seldom acknowledged, the linguistic and cultural bridges these slaves navigated added another layer of complexity to their existence. Ripped from diverse backgrounds across the Caucasus, they were thrust into a world where understanding the language of their captors became a matter of survival. Whether communicating in hushed tones in the kitchens or obeying shouted commands in the fields, mastering the speech of the Ottomans was yet another silent form of subjugation.

In some rare instances, a slave's skill could elevate them to somewhat better circumstances. Talented craftsmen, musicians, or those with specialized agricultural skills found their conditions slightly improved. Yet, even this acknowledgment of their abilities existed within the strict confines of their roles as property. Such "privileges" were granted not out of kindness, but from sheer utilitarian need. Talent became another chain, albeit gilded, binding them to their masters' whims.

The haunting legacy of this plantation life and domestic servitude reverberates through the annals of history. It underlines the harrowing resilience of those whose lives were confined to relentless labor. From the boundless wilderness of the fields to the constricted corners of households, these slaves endured an existence of ceaseless labor, silent resistance, fleeting hopes, and unwavering despair. Their plight paints a tableau both stark and nuanced, immortalized by the very resilience with which they endured it.

Inhumane Treatment and Punishments

The plight of slaves in the Ottoman Empire is a narrative steeped in relentless suffering, cloaked in shadows and echoed within the walls of grand palaces and lowly huts alike. The institution of slavery in this era, particularly concerning Caucasian captives, was characterized by a level of cruelty that bespoke an order devoid of compassion. The Ottoman masters wielded their authority with a hand of iron, often dispensing brutality as a testament to their power.

Punishments were manifold and executed with an oft monstrous ingenuity that bespoke the regime's insatiable hunger for dominance. Physical abuse, of course, was but the everyday bread of the oppressed. Whips and canes lashed the flesh of men, women, and children, leaving behind scars that could be read like a grim diary of agony. The sound of the whip cracking through the air, followed by the inevitable scream, was an almost ritualistic undertaking, meant to cow others into obedience.

One might think that this overt display of muscle was sufficient to maintain control, but no; the cruelty extended beyond the corporeal. Many slaves found themselves strung up by their hands or feet, subjected to public humiliation. It was not uncommon for recalcitrant slaves to be paraded through towns, their crimes broadcasted as a morose warning to others. Public executions were a particularly grim spectacle, serving as both entertainment and edification for the masses.

For those who dared to entertain thoughts of escape, the consequences were dire. The Ottoman system had mastered psychological warfare; tales of recaptured slaves circulated like wildfire. The unlucky ones had their Achilles tendons severed, making a second flight an impossible dream. Some were blinded or had their ears lopped off, forced to wander the streets as living reminders of the futility of rebellion.

There was a darker layer still, hidden from the public eye, where the walls of harems and palaces housed unspeakable torment. Female slaves often bore the brunt of this hidden cruelty. Abused not only as laborers but also as objects of desire, many faced a daily horror that words can scarce encapsulate. The presence of eunuchs, themselves victims of emasculation and endless indignity, cast a somber light on the twisted practices sanctioned within those walls.

If physical and psychological punishments were not enough, the master's dominion extended even into spiritual realms. Forced conversion to Islam was used as a tool to obliterate the very identity of the enslaved. Those who resisted faced even harsher treatments, sometimes executed by methods meant to instill religious overtones—burned alive, flayed, or even crucified.

The slave market was another site of dehumanization. Potential buyers inspected the enslaved like livestock, poking and prodding, checking teeth and muscle, as the slaves stood naked and trembling. The psychological toll of being reduced to mere chattel cannot be overstated. Many were separated from their families, sold off to distant lands, where hope and familiarity became foreign concepts.

Some slave owners delighted in more elaborate forms of torment— luckless souls found themselves chained for days, deprived of food and water. Choking dehydration or the slow grip of starvation was a tactical, almost surgical method of breaking a spirit. These prolonged afflictions were Pagean plays of sadistic artistry, endeavors in creating living sculptures of despair.

Sadism took on many forms, each one more refined, more unpalatable, than the last. Some enslaved souls were forced to carry out tasks laced with peril, tasks that put their very lives at risk. Felling trees in hazardous conditions, mining under treacherous earth, and even being dispatched on suicidal errands under the guise of loyalty—the specter of death was a constant companion.

Many of these tales, buried deep within layers of history, struggle to see the light of day. It is as though the earth itself seeks to hush these sorrowful whispers. Yet, it is crucial to unearth these grim relics and confront the collective memory of humanity with them. The dark shadows of inhumane treatment and punishment stand as grim milestones upon the path of human history, reminders of ignominy that must never be tread again.

Diseases from untreated wounds, malnutrition, and relentless toil claimed innumerable lives. There were no reprieves, nor any semblance of mercy. For every laborer weakened by drudgery, an iron manacle awaited. These manacles wore not just on flesh and bone but sank deeply into the sinews of the mind, a constant reminder that liberty was a privilege long lost.

However, there was rarely peace found even in death. It wasn't uncommon for the desecration of a slave's remains to serve as another form of punishment, a final indignity heaped upon a suffering soul. Bodies were left to rot in the open, displayed as festering trophies of submission. The anonimity of these souls has turned their stories into ghostly whispers, still haunting those ruins of crumbled empires.

The Ottoman slave system's insidious nature extended even to young children who were forcefully conscripted into the Janissary corps—a stark deviation from a life that should have been filled with innocence and familial warmth. Once inducted, their childhood dissipated into rigor and martial discipline, foregoing tenderness for the deadly art of war. This was another dimension of punishment, the slow theft of what could have been a form of joyful normalcy.

It is vital for the annals of historical scholarship to dwell upon these grievous tales. The ghostly echoes of inhumanity and cruelty form an essential part of our understanding of past societies, cautioning us against the repetition of such vile acts. Historians must therefore act as both custodians and exorcists, preserving these sorrowful narratives while expelling the malignance that they represent from our present and future.

Though time has lent a verdant shroud to these atrocities, letting new generations tread upon the grounds where unspeakable tragedies once occurred, one must never forget the echoes of the wretched. The images of bindings and whips, the silence imposed by fear, the myriad forms of suffering inflicted without remorse or reprieve—these stand as monuments to a past that, while shadowed and grim, must be confronted in its entirety.

Through this confrontation, it is hoped the veils of ignorance could be lifted, healing the festering wounds history has inflicted upon itself. Allowing the world to remember, to weep, and ultimately to garner the strength and will to fervently say: Never again.

Chapter 4: The Economic Impact of Slavery on the Ottoman Empire

Underneath the gilded splendor of the Ottoman Empire's wealth lies a foundation built upon the suffering of enslaved souls. This economic engine, driven by the relentless churn of human bondage, girded the empire's coffers with a dark, unyielding force. Vast markets from Constantinople to Cairo bustled with the dehumanizing transactions that filled the empire's treasury, each auction manifesting the grim reality of commodified lives. Slavery wasn't merely a social ill but an intrinsic part of the Ottoman economic edifice, with many regions heavily dependent on the labor and revenue generated by this abhorrent practice. The empire's growth, often marveled at from afar, was entwined with the procurement, trade, and exploitation of both men and women, whose lives were consumed in the furnace of imperial ambition. Far from being an isolated atrocity, slavery's economic threads wove through the empire's very fabric, dictating policies, war strategies, and trade routes. The fiscal might and splendor that dazzled the Western world came at the cost of countless lives, rendered invisible by the seductive glint of gold and power.

Revenue from Slave Markets

In the shadowed alleys and bustling bazaars of the Ottoman Empire, the slave markets stood as grim pillars of economic gain, casting long and morose shadows over the region's prosperity. From the moment they were violently uprooted from their homelands, these unfortunate souls became commodities, their worth measured in gold and silver. The major slave markets, located in cities such as Istanbul and Cairo, pulsated with the sinister transactions that fed the Empire's coffers. The incessant demand for labor, particularly in domestic and agricultural roles, meant that the market for Caucasian slaves remained fiercely lucrative. The revenue generated from this human chattel not only propped up the Ottoman economy but also funded various endeavors of the state, creating an abhorrent cycle of dependency that intertwined the Empire's opulence with the suffering of countless enslaved individuals.

Major Slave Markets and Their Operations loomed large as macabre theaters in the dark tragedy of Caucasian slavery. Within these infernal bazaars, the human form transformed into a mere commodity, as souls were bartered and sold under the steely gaze of Ottoman overseers. From the grand cities of Istanbul and Algiers to the lesser-known outposts along the North African coast, these markets functioned as the nerve centers of a sprawling trade, their operations slick with the grease of human suffering.

The principal markets thrived where the sands of Africa kissed the Mediterranean shores. Istanbul, the magnificent capital of the Ottoman Empire, was a bustling hub where slaves of all origins were traded. This cosmopolitan metropolis bore witness to unspeakable scenes, as captives —young and old, noble and common—were paraded before potential buyers, their fates hanging in the balance like livestock at auction. The air thick with incense could not mask the stench of misery emanating from the pens where these unfortunates were held.

Algiers, another significant node, thrummed with activity, its docks bustling with ships brimming with human cargo. This pirate enclave, a notorious bastion of the Barbary corsairs, held weekly markets where the cries of the enslaved echoed through the narrow, winding alleys like mournful dirges. European captives found themselves displayed like trophies, their pale complexions fetching higher prices compared to their darker-skinned counterparts. Such was the paradox of value and devaluation interwoven within the very fabric of these infernal transactions.

The structure of these markets was frightfully methodical. Each auction day would begin with a public display, the captives placed on a raised platform for the scrutiny of potential buyers. Traders and affluent patrons mingled, inspecting the pallor and muscle of each individual, their keen eyes assessing the worth of each bicep, each set of teeth. The cacophony of voices rising in bid echoed the crescendo of despair that permeated these proceedings. After the sale, new masters claimed their chattel, often branding them as property in a painful ritual that signified their new, debased existence.

The peripheral markets in towns like Tripoli and Tunis also played vital roles. Smaller in scale but equally dreadful in their purpose, these outposts provided vital supply lines feeding the voracious demands of larger cities. Raiders would transport their captives across treacherous terrain, often losing many to exhaustion, disease, or ruthless execution. Those who survived the journey entered these secondary markets already battered by the elements and hardship, only to face an uncertain fate.

The operations were overseen by appointed officials and slave merchants who ensured the smooth functioning of this enterprise. These administrators upheld an intricate system of accounting and inventory, meticulously recording each transaction. The intricacies of the financial mechanisms supporting these markets were designed to maximize profit while minimizing loss, with each life's worth reduced to mere lines in ledgers, chillingly efficient and devoid of empathy.

Yet, beneath this layer of methodical cruelty lay a labyrinth of deceit and subterfuge. Corruption was rampant, greased palms a common sight as bribes flowed freely to secure favorable transactions or to spirit away coveted captives. A dark undercurrent of escaped slaves and rebels further complicated matters, as underground networks formed to rescue those trapped within this malign system. Disguises and forged documents circulated, and clandestine meetings took place under the murky cloak of night, highlighting the constant tension between oppressors and the oppressed.

Not all markets were identical in their operation; each had its own macabre specialties. Some catered to the agricultural demands of the Empire, providing laborers for the vast estates and farms that dotted the landscape. Others supplied the domestic needs of wealthy households, selecting individuals with perceived sartorial grace and obedience. There were markets for those destined to serve in military capacities, rigorously trained as soldiers, or even specialized in eunuchs—grotesquely prized for their supposed loyalty and docility.

The value of a slave varied drastically based on age, physical condition, and skills. Young women, often subjected to the vile gazes and lecherous hands of their purchasers, were highly sought after, especially for roles in harems or as personal attendants. Men with robust physiques, deemed fit for labor, commanded substantial sums. Children, heartbreaking in their innocence, were seen as long-term investments, malleable and easier to indoctrinate to their deplorable fates. Each demographic group had its price, calculated with chilling precision in the dark parlance of these grim marketplaces.

Despite the bleakness, acts of resistance did occur within these markets. Some slaves attempted daring escapes, often aligning with sympathetic locals or even fellow captives. Tales of revolt sprouted like grim roses amidst the desert of desolation; some would take up arms or fabricate dangerous lies to hinder their oppressors' plans. Though largely unsuccessful in altering the broader institution, these acts of defiance served as poignant reminders of the undying spirit of those trapped within such horrid commerce.

In the aftermath of each market day, the ramifications reverberated through the Ottoman economy. The revenue generated from these transactions fed back into the imperial coffers, financing further military campaigns and luxurious lifestyles for the elite. The human machinery driving the Ottoman Empire's economic engine was lubricated with the blood and sweat of its most downtrodden, an appalling nexus of commerce and cruelty that underpinned much of its wealth. It is perhaps here where the true horror resides—not just in the act of enslavement but in the systemic incorporation of human misery into the very fabric of an empire's prosperity.

Thus, we see that the operations of these major slave markets were meticulously planned and systematically cruel. The rot that lay at the heart of this slavery seeped into every corner of Ottoman society, a dark chapter in history underscored by the relentless buying and selling of human beings. To study these markets is to peer into the abyss, to behold the raw machinery of human degradation operating at full tilt, lubricated by greed and perpetuated by the indifferent machinations of power.

Economic Dependencies and Growth

The Ottoman Empire, vast and complex, wove slavery into the very fabric of its economy. Their reliance on slave labor formed an intricate web of dependencies, driving both commerce and social structures. This symbiotic relationship, parasitic yet foundational, was not merely incidental but rather emblematic of the empire's economic framework.

In the bustling bazaars and clandestine markets, the chink of coins echoed the fate of Caucasian slaves. The coffers of the Empire swelled; Sultanates and Viziers grew fat on the profits derived from human chattel. Yet, behind this veneer of prosperity lurked a darker reality. The very lifeblood of this economy, the slaves, existed in a liminal space between commodity and human, a torturous duality.

Economic dependencies extended far beyond the initial transaction. The Ottoman economy absorbed slaves into various sectors - agriculture, military, and domestic spheres. The agricultural fields, heavy with the yield of coerced labor, symbolized a grim juxtaposition: fertile lands irrigated not just by water but by the sweat and blood of enslaved souls. Here, labor was extracted, brutal and relentless, under the unyielding gaze of overseers.

The military, too, drew upon these captive bodies. The infamous Janissaries are one poignant example. Originally composed of young Christian boys, forcibly converted and trained, they metamorphosed into elites. This peculiar system of forced conscription, known as the Devshirme, created a military class both dependent on and loyal to the Sultanate. Slavery thus seeped into the sinews of the state's defense mechanisms, ensuring both its safeguarding and perpetuation.

Domestically, within the labyrinthine corridors of Ottoman palaces and mansions, slaves performed myriad roles. From menial tasks to intricate courtly duties, the reach of slavery permeated every crevice of domestic life. The opulent silks and sumptuous foods enjoyed by the Ottoman elite were procured through the deft hands of those in chains. This domestic dependence fostered an environment where the presence of slavery was normalized, insidiously invisible yet ubiquitously felt.

While the immediate economic benefits of slavery were palpable, the long-term ramifications cannot be ignored. The reliance on slave labor stunted technological advancements and innovations. The availability of cheap, coerced labor obviated the need for mechanization or productivity improvements. Economically, this dependency sowed the seeds of stagnation, an irony writ large upon the annals of history.

Moreover, the economic growth fueled by slavery was a double-edged sword. In the short term, revenues flourished, and the empire expanded its territories. Slave trade routes and markets became pivotal nodes of economic activity, drawing wealth into the Ottoman treasury. But this growth rested on precarious foundations. The human cost was immense, and the social volatility it engendered left the empire vulnerable to both internal dissent and external condemnation.

The reverberations of this economic model echoed through the various strata of Ottoman society. Wealth accumulated in the hands of few, creating a stark disparity between the elite and the rest. This economic chasm, widened by the labor of slaves, fostered resentment and unrest—a powder keg of social tensions waiting to erupt.

Furthermore, the economic dependencies fed into a vicious cycle of supply and demand. As the empire's territories expanded, so did its need for slaves, setting off a relentless pursuit for more captives. This relentless demand spurred raids, wars, and even treaties designed not to quell slavery but to secure steady supplies of human labor. The very treaties that professed peace often veiled the sinister agreements fuelled by avarice.

In examining this economic dependence, one must not overlook the spiritual and moral decay it wrought. The commodification of human beings dehumanized not just the slaves but also those who profited from and perpetuated the system. The moral corrosion permeated society, intertwining economic prosperity with ethical bankruptcy, an inescapable paradox.

Yet, the Ottomans were not unique in this plight. Their narrative of economic dependencies and growth mirrored other empires whose golden eras were drenched in the suffering of the subjugated. However, the Ottoman manifestation was distinct in its scale and systemic integration of slavery across all facets of economic life.

One can't overstate the complexities of these dependencies. The gruesome cycle of enslavement and exploitation necessitated a labyrinthine network of intermediaries, each profiting from the human misery that underpinned the Ottoman economy. Traders, brokers, and transporters—all knaves in this nefarious chain—contributed to an economy where human dignity was bartered daily.

Amidst this bleak tableau, some glimmers of resistance emerged, both subtle and overt. Enslaved individuals, though trapped in an oppressive economic system, found ways to subvert and challenge their plight. Acts of resistance—whether through escape, sabotage, or insurrection—acted as counter-narratives, though seldom successful, to the hegemonic economic dependencies.

Historians and economists alike must grapple with the legacies of such dependencies. The Ottoman Empire's reliance on slavery was both its strength and Achilles' heel. The initial economic gains masked a gradual erosion of moral and social coherence. Indeed, the economic growth driven by slavery bore fruits that were, in many ways, poisoned.

In summation, the economic dependencies and growth tied to slavery in the Ottoman Empire present a harrowing tale. It's a narrative of wealth built on agony, of progress shackled by inhumanity. This complex interplay between economic gain and ethical compromise stands as a sobering reminder of the costs of such dependencies. As we uncover these layers, we bear witness to a saga where economic dependencies fostered growth but left an indelible scar on the very soul of the Empire.

Chapter 5: The Social Hierarchy and Roles of Slaves

In the labyrinthine strata of Ottoman society, the existence of Caucasian slaves was both paradoxical and emblematic of an era rife with contradiction. These souls, ripped from homelands and thrust into unfamiliar terrains, found their fates variably tethered to the whims of their masters. Some endured backbreaking toils in the rural expanses, where the harsh elements became both adversary and overseer. Others, ensnared in urban sprawls, navigated the intricate lattice of serving within households adorned with opulence they could never claim. The roles assigned to these unfortunates were manifold: concubines, eunuchs, and laborers—each role a cog in the vast, merciless machinery of the empire. Yet, within this rigid hierarchy, whispers of resistance brewed, a testament to the indomitable human spirit yearning for freedom. The social fabric, though seemingly resilient, bore the silent scars of these subjugated lives, marking an insidious legacy that historians unravel thread by painful thread.

Integration into Ottoman Society

The Caucasian slaves, forcibly integrated into the vast expanse of the Ottoman societal framework, found themselves navigating intricate webs of servitude and sporadic opportunity. While many languished in arduous labor, some seized the chance to ascend the ranks through service in elite households or the military, thereby perpetuating a paradox of subjugation and conditional privilege. The city streets and remote hinterlands alike bore witness to these chameleonic existences, where slaves might toil under the watchful eyes of their masters or subtly influence the corridors of power. Amidst the opulence and rigor of the Ottoman milieu, the integration was less a seamless union and more a juxtaposition of worlds —one anchored in the relentless grip of bondage, the other occasionally yielding a slender escape from the relentlessness of their plight. This duality underscored the complex tapestry of Ottoman society, wherein the presence of Caucasian slaves was both a glaring testament to human suffering and an understated narrative of resilience and adaptation.

Differences Between Urban and Rural Slaves within the sprawling and intricate web of Ottoman society present a vivid tableau of contrasts, both in their day-to-day toil and in the textures of their suffering. The sentences etched in the hallowed annals of history portray an existence as dissimilar as city and countryside, sharply delineated by the walls that encapsulated their respective fates.

Urban slaves, confined within the bustling cities of the Ottoman Empire, often found themselves in tightly packed quarters and subject to the watchful eyes of their masters. They performed various tasks, many of which were closely linked with household duties and personal service. Among the daily rituals of preparing meals, cleaning, and serving their masters, these slaves often had to maintain an incessant air of subservience, a mask that concealed their true despair. The conditioning of close contact with their masters and the urban elite could sometimes foster a more nuanced relationship, occasionally punctuated with moments of leniency, yet never truly liberated from the iron grip of servitude.

The urban atmosphere was one of relentless activity where the clangor of commerce and the din of trade routes underscored their servile endeavors. Their labor often extended into the echelons of craftsmanship, where some were trained as artisans, cooks, tailors, or even administrative aides. However, proficiency in these trades did not equate to freedom but rather forged new chains of dependency, binding them even tighter to their masters' wills. The loquacious markets and opulent households underscored a façade of civilization that belied the brutal reality of their enslavement.

In stark contrast, rural slaves were cast upon the expansive, often unforgiving landscapes of the Ottoman tributaries, engaged in backbreaking labor under the unrelenting sun. Their existence was marked by an arduous routine—from the first light of dawn to the encroaching twilight—working the fields, tending to livestock, and grappling with the elements. The pastoral environs, romanticized in literature and art, were a prison unto their own, their beauty marred by the agony and exhaustion of those who toiled upon them.

Separated from the relative hustle of urban centers, rural slaves often faced harsher, more isolated conditions. The expanse of the landscape rendered policing more sporadic yet paradoxically more brutal when it manifested. The physicality of agrarian labor demanded not just endurance, but the forfeit of one's spirit and will. These slaves were often under the strict control of landowners who saw them merely as expendable tools for enhancing their agricultural yield, devoid of even the faintest glimmer of humanity.

The isolation fostered by the rural setting also led to significant differences in social interactions. Unlike their urban counterparts who might find solace in the sporadic camaraderie of other household slaves or fleeting kindnesses from city folk, rural slaves were profoundly estranged from such human interactions. Their lives were often consumed by a haunting solitude, the only voices being those of their masters or the cries of their fellow laborers, carried away by the winds over the fields.

Urban slaves sometimes had access to basic literacy and education, often as a means of better serving their masters in more complex tasks. This slight boon held the irony of empowerment imprisoned within the cage of dependency. Masters utilized the educated slave's knowledge for personal gains in trade, finance, or administration, their capabilities never truly inuring to their own benefit.

Conversely, rural slaves seldom saw the inside of a book or enjoyed the luxury of formal education. Their world revolved around the cycles of planting, tending, and harvesting. The seasons dictated their work, binding them to a relentless calendar that neither advised nor advanced them. Their intellectual destitution paralleled the barrenness of their freedom, an existence shaped by neither learning nor liberation.

Diet and sustenance also drew a line of disparity. Urban slaves, though tasked with food preparation, often partook in the leftovers of their masters, occasionally enjoying richer fare but more typically surviving on sparse rations. The variety available in bustling markets sometimes trickled down to them, offering a modest reprieve from their culinary monotony. Yet, such instances were rare and punctuated by long periods of insufficiency.

In contrast, rural slaves' diets were even more meager and monotonous, sustained largely on seasonal produce and scant rations provided by the landowners. They reaped no benefit from the labor they invested in the soil. Their meals, often as plain and uncaring as their masters' attitudes, barely sufficed to sustain the energy required for their relentless physical exertion.

Despite these differences, a unifying chord of oppression bound them, articulated through manifold means of punishment and control. Both urban and rural slaves were subject to the capricious cruelties of their masters. Urban households wielded punishments that were immediate and often publicly degrading, leveraging social visibility to enforce compliance. On the other hand, rural punishments, while less visible, were brutal in their severity, meant to serve as dire warnings to others.

Thus, while their surroundings and specific duties diverged markedly, the essence of their plight remained tragically consistent. Neither the proximity to culture and commerce in urban centers nor the isolation within the expansive rural domains provided any sanctuary from the perpetual bondage that characterized their existence. Whether hemmed in by the stone walls of cities or lost to the infinite horizon of the fields, their souls were equally fettered, their lives testimony to a shared, vast, and unmitigated sorrow.

Resistance and Rebellion

The annals of history bear testament to a truth as old as time itself—
wherever oppression festers, resistance inevitably rises in defiance. The
enslaved Caucasians within the Ottoman Empire were no exception to this
immutable law. Stripped of their homes and herded into foreign lands,
their spirits often blazed defiantly against the chains that bound them.
These instances of rebellion and insurgence, though varied in form and
efficacy, were ever-present throbs of life amidst a sea of subjugation.

For many, the seeds of rebellion were sown within the heart of their
despair. The most palpable acts of resistance emerged from an amalgam
of profound hopelessness and fleeting opportunities. Among the most
daring were the conspiracies forged in the dim-lit quarters of urban
slaves. These clandestine gatherings concocted plans as intricate as any
political intrigue, aiming to overthrow the shackles of their oppressors. In
cities where slaves were relegated to domestic roles, they seized chances
born of proximity, exploiting their knowledge of household routines and
the structural weaknesses of their captors' residences.

In stark contrast, the rebellions within rural domains unfolded less subtly,
marked by sudden outbursts of violence. Here, the rigors of agricultural
labor bred robust and desperate souls. The hope of reclaiming freedom
pushed these slaves toward open revolts. Armed with tools of their toil,
they confronted overseers and sometimes even retreated into the wild,
attempting to carve out transient sanctuaries where Ottoman reach
faltered. The remote landscapes provided both refuge and peril, for the
eyes of hunters and informants lurked even within the shelter of the
forests.

These acts of overt defiance were not the sole avenues of resistance. The
Caucasian slaves engaged in subtler, yet equally potent, means of
rebellion. Sabotage became their silent creed; from disrupting the
machinery of their servitude to poisoning the provisions of their masters,
such acts were whispers of dissent in the bedlam of oppression. These

actions, though often evanescent and seen by the oppressors as mere nuisances, were veritable assertions of agency and humanity.

The psychological rebellion among slaves, though less visible, wove itself deeply into the fabric of their existence. Maintaining cultural identity became an act of resistance. Through the clandestine practice of their native customs and the quiet preservation of their languages amidst the alien culture of the Ottoman Empire, slaves inscribed their unyielding spirit into the annals of time. These small acts of defiance formed an intrinsic bulwark against the erasure of their histories and identities.

Yet, the chronicles of darkest resistance reached their zenith in the organized insurrections, where collective action forged ephemeral respites from bondage. The grandest, though seldom successful, were insurrections that sent tremors through the Empire. Panicked whispers of such revolts rippled through the slave populace, igniting glimmers of hope. Accounts of escaped slaves who had mustered into guerrilla bands abounded, their tales growing into legends that would stoke the fires of rebellion in the hearts of the oppressed.

One such insurrection, indelibly etched in the annals of resistance, transpired in the battered yet unbowed enclave of Odesa. The slaves, honing their defiance through years of insidious acts of sabotage, culminated their insurgency by orchestrating a coordinated assault against their captors. Though ultimately quashed, the revolt left an indelible mark, serving as both caution and inspiration for those who remained in chains.

It must not be understated that these acts of rebellion carried with them grave repercussions. Harsh reprisals were the norm, and the specter of punishment loomed over every seditious whisper or act. Public executions, floggings, and torture were employed to maintain an iron grip on the seditious souls. The brutal quelling of these rebellions served as a dire warning to others, though it simultaneously sowed seeds of deeper animosity and desperation.

Alliances also played an instrumental role in the resistance narrative. Bonded by their shared plight, slaves sometimes managed to forge unlikely coalitions with free but discontented factions within the Ottoman society, including rival ethnic groups and fallen courtiers. These unlikely alliances rendered their insurgencies more formidable. While temporary, these joint efforts left lasting impressions and incited further insubordination.

The spiritual bastion of faith also bolstered resistance. Christian slaves often sought solace and solidarity in their shared religion, forming secret congregations. Prayers, hymns, and clandestine masses became acts of spiritual defiance against their Muslim captors. These assemblies were not merely for worship; they were vital networks through which news, plans, and morale were circulated. Faith intertwined with resistance, and in this, many found the strength to endure and continue their seditious endeavors.

Resistance was not confined to the corporeal realm alone; intellectual defiance was a potent tool wielded by the more educated captives. The enslaved scribes and scholars used their literacy to forge falsified documents, craft letters of dissent, and disseminate revolutionary ideas. Their writings, smuggled through covert channels, ignited intellectual rebellions that echoed through the minds of the enslaved and free alike. The pen, as is often said, proved mightier than the sword.

As we delve deeper into the labyrinth of resistance, let us not lose sight of the broader sociopolitical milieu that shaped these rebellions. The tides of rebellion were influenced by the currents of power and policy within the Ottoman Empire. Shifts in administrative focus, wars, and economic pressures often created fissures within which acts of rebellion could take root. Understanding these broader factors provides a canvas upon which the strokes of insurgent acts are vividly painted.

In the grand tapestry of history, the resistance and rebellion of Caucasian slaves in the Ottoman Empire occupy a place of enduring significance. These acts, both grand and subtle, were emblematic of an indomitable human spirit that refused to succumb to the inexorable march of oppression. Their legacy, though often eclipsed by the annals of their more numerous African counterparts, remains a poignant chapter in the saga of human resilience.

Theirs was a struggle that transcended the mere quest for freedom; it was a rebellion against the very essence of dehumanization. Every act of rebellion, whether it ended in fleeting liberty or dire consequence, carved out a space for future generations to dream of emancipation. This resistance, imbued with a shadowed nobility, whispers through the corridors of history, echoing the timeless human yearning for dignity and freedom.

In closing, let us remember that these acts of insurgency and defiance by Caucasian slaves were more than mere historical footnotes. They serve as enduring testaments to the unquenchable fire of the human spirit. These stories of resistance and rebellion beckon us to ponder deeply on the nature of freedom and the lengths to which the oppressed will go to reclaim their humanity.

Chapter 6: European Reactions and Responses

As the spectral grip of Ottoman chains tightened on the hapless Caucasian captives, the reaction from European shores grew ever more fervent. Diplomatic entreaties swelled with the urgency of familial wails, each missive bearing the weight of a continent's ransom demands and desperate treaties. In the murky alleyways of burgeoning European cities, tales of abductions and enslavement were recounted in hushed tones over flickering candlelight, casting elongated shadows on crumbling walls as visceral outrage mingled with paralyzing fear. Media of the age, from pamphleteers to the earliest broadsheets, inked in bold declarations, transformed communal horror into a clarion call for action. The prevailing public sentiment veered between impassioned crusades for freedom and the cold machinations of political strategists, each portraying a continent on the cusp of moral and cultural reckoning. Europe's collective conscience grappled with the abominable reality— forcing kingdoms and principalities alike to chart precarious courses through the waters of diplomacy and the stormy gales of public opinion.

Diplomatic Efforts to End Slavery

The harrowing epoch of Caucasian slavery, entrenched in the ruthless grip of the Ottoman Empire, elicited fervent diplomatic maneuvers among European nations, each orchestrating a symphony of treaties and negotiations, scenes as layered as the darkest tragedies. Diplomatic envoys, draped in layers of intrigue and desperation, wove complex tapestries of ransoms and accords, determined to extricate their compatriots from the clutches of barbaric servitude. Ludicrous demands and extravagant promises exchanged under foreboding skies, illuminated only by fleeting hope. The evolving dance between European emissaries and Ottoman dignitaries was not merely a clash of civilizations; it was an existential struggle, a desperate ballet where missteps could spell doom for countless souls. This diplomatic ballet was conducted in shadowy chambers and on blood-stained battlegrounds, with every act weighed down by the palpable weight of human despair and resilient defiance, echoing through corridors of power like ghostly laments of forgotten generations.

Treaties and Ransoms bear witness to an era marred by the relentless bargaining for human lives, a dark cadence danced between European states and the Ottoman Empire. As the Barbary Pirates intercepted vessels upon the high seas, the cold clink of chains and the despairing cries of newly captured souls signaled the beginning of a grueling ordeal. But the story didn't end there. Between the loss of freedom and the rare glimmer of liberation lay a web of treaties and ransoms negotiated with the hopes of restoring liberty to the unfortunate captives.

European nations, confronted by the persistent threat of piracy and enslavement, often found themselves coerced into diplomatic dialogues with the Ottoman rulers and Barbary states. In these discussions, the captives became currency. It was not uncommon for states to engage in lengthy negotiations, offering gold, weapons, or other treasures in exchange for their people. The process was fraught with complexity and frailty, often hinging on the states' ability to pay the demanded ransoms and the pirates' willingness to release the captives.

Historical documents from the 16th and 17th centuries are replete with accounts of treaties aimed at curtailing piracy and slavery. These agreements, albeit fragile, served as temporary shields for European merchants and seafarers. One prominent example is the treaty between England and the Ottoman Empire, which sought to ensure the safe passage of English vessels through the treacherous waters of the Mediterranean. It is within these edicts that the desperation and resilience of states are most evident, as entire councils convened to debate the merits of paying vast sums for the return of their countrymen.

Ransoms, the monetary lifeline for imprisoned souls, often required organized efforts led by religious and charitable organizations. The Catholic Church, for instance, established orders specifically tasked with the redemption of captives. The Trinitarians and Mercedarians worked tirelessly, traversing dangerous territories and negotiating with their captors to secure release. Such missions required not just silver and gold, but also the sheer will and bravery of the intermediaries who risked their own freedom to save others.

The plight of the enslaved was exacerbated by the socio-political landscape of the time, where ransom negotiations were perilously dependent on the fluctuating tides of alliance and enmity. A change in leadership, war, or even minor diplomatic squabbles could prolong a captive's suffering indefinitely. Many captives found themselves languishing for years, their fates swinging like delicate threads in the wind.

While some ransoms were successful, others faltered, not due to lack of negotiation but because of sheer impoverishment of the state or the high demand set by the pirates. It is here that the tales of those left behind evoke a somber resonance. Records reveal the harrowing accounts of families selling their belongings, towns rallying to collect funds, and governments incurring significant debts—all in the hope of reuniting with their loved ones. These stark realities underscore the severe agony and length to which individuals and communities went to redeem kin and compatriots.

The Treaty of Aranjuez of 1787 between Spain and Morocco is another pertinent example. This agreement, both intricate and painstaking, illustrated the delicate balance of diplomacy. Spain, reeling from recurrent pirate attacks, sought a mutual understanding to mitigate the threat. The ensuing truce permitted freed captives to return home, bolstering a sense of tentative relief among Spanish citizens. However, such treaties often faced challenges in enforcement and adherence, rendering them susceptible to breaches that reignited conflict and captivity.

Unexpected alliances frequently emerged as states discovered shared interests in eliminating the piracy scourge. Joint naval expeditions and partnership treaties became more commonplace, revealing a collective effort to curb the endemic threat. Yet the intricacy of these arrangements often meant that true resolution remained elusive. The pirates, ever resourceful and incentivized by the lucrative ransoms, adapted their strategies to evade suppression.

Ransoming extended beyond mere financial exchange. It assumed a form of psychological warfare, where captors would disseminate letters from prisoners to their homeland, filled with pleas for rescue and descriptions of their suffering. This tactic applied pressure to the families and governments, accentuating the urgency of payment. The emotional torment intertwined with this process laid bare the human cost of the ordeal, adding depth to the historical narrative of Caucasian slavery.

Moreover, certain treaties stipulated terms for the humane treatment of captives. These clauses, while rarely adhered to in full, reflected an early attempt to introduce a semblance of ethical conduct in an otherwise brutal system. The interweaving of ethics with diplomacy in these contexts highlights the struggle to balance pragmatism with humanity during such dire circumstances.

- The Treaty of Peace and Commerce negotiated by France in 1683 exemplifies efforts to institute more humane conditions. While primarily aimed at economic balance, it incorporated specific provisions addressing the treatment of French captives, indicating a progressive shift in diplomatic priorities.
- Similarly, the Treaty of Carlowitz (1699), while broadly focusing on territorial agreements, embedded clauses that hinted at concerns over slavery and ransoms, demonstrating the layered complexity of diplomatic engagements during this era.

Ultimately, the combination of treaties and ransoms represents a dual-faceted approach to addressing the hardship of enslavement. These forced diplomatic engagements mirrored the relentless struggle between survival and subjugation, liberty and bondage. The complex interplay between power, wealth, and human resilience is at the heart of this narrative, rendering "Treaties and Ransoms" a poignant chapter in the history of Caucasian slavery within the Ottoman Empire.

Notwithstanding the occasional successes, the ceaseless demand for ransoms and the transient nature of treaties etched a world perennially at the mercy of merciless corsairs. Each agreement and ransom story serves as an indelible testament to the fragility and constant flux of human freedom during this turbulent epoch. While some captives were fortunate to see the shores of their homeland again, many lingered in an enduring limbo, their fates wrapped tightly within the shifting sands of diplomacy.

Public Perception and Media Coverage

Throughout the annals of time, public perception has often swayed like the pendulum of an ancient clock, ticking away in tune with the breath of prevailing winds. Europeans of the 16th and 17th centuries found themselves ensnared not only by the ravages of the Ottoman Empire but also by the tales of those ravages, equally enlivening and horrifying. The media of the era, in its rudimentary yet potent form, played a principal role in shaping the collective consciousness.

Print media, burgeoning in its infancy, carried the ink-stained testimonies of anguished survivors. Pamphlets, broadsheets, and ballads became the messengers of dire news. These graphic accounts of raids and captures by the Barbary pirates spread like wildfire through the cobbled streets of Europe. Whether tales exacted from liberated captives or the melancholic verses of an anonymous poet, the media crafted a spectral visage of Oriental savagery.

Particularly in seafaring nations such as Spain, England, and the Netherlands, the imagery of white slavery conjured a public outcry, arousing both fear and fervent nationalism. Stories recounted families torn asunder, men fettered and dragged into foreign servitude, and women enduring unutterable trials. Simplistic and sensationalist though some narratives were, they highlighted the dread and contempt Europeans held towards their distant foes.

Might it be considered that this cacophony of anxiety-induced fervor was but a prelude to wider diplomatic stratagems? Indeed, government-aligned scribes and clandestine propagandists fanned the embers of public perception, aligning it with the winds of statecraft. Treatises, some penned under the quill of the elite, became instruments for rallying support for anti-Ottoman expeditions, ransoms, and rescue missions. Diplomatic chess played out on an increasingly visible stage, sanctioned by the court of public opinion.

Howbeit, not all print was afforded by noble distress. Journalists and street poets, driven by commercial or altruistic design, mingled reportage with critique. Therein lay a burgeoning skepticism towards the ruling class's response — or perceived lack thereof — to the plight of enslaved peers. Underground pamphleteers would mockingly question, "What coin is paid for honor reclaimed when captives remain unredeemed?" The populace, caught in the delicate dance of credence and scorn, oscillated in their faith in their sovereigns.

The harrowing picture painted by these media often melded with the artistic sensibilities of the era. Paintings, sketches, and etchings would cipher the tales of torment into visual lore. Artists, both famed and obscure, would emblazon their canvases with the monochrome misery and muted glory of captured Europeans, shackled and mournful in alien lands. Such works did not merely adorn homes and halls; they modeled the public's understanding and emotional receptivity, oftentimes casting slaves as the tragic heroes of an indefinite twilight.

In the eyes of Europe's literati, from Marlowe to Molière, the Ottoman yoke offered rich fodder for allegory and critique. Plays and literary works dramatized the European affliction, merging it with the zeitgeist's undulating fears and fantasies. Theatre aficionados would thus sit enraptured as the plights of captives unfurled upon the stage, stirring their own emotions and prejudices into a fervent broth. Scribes captured not mere lamentations but also expressions of redemption, resistance, and moral quandary, thereby lending a complex resonance to the discourse.

Were we to traverse the cobbled streets and bustling courts of Europe, one would undeniably find whispered conversations, tavern tales, and sermonized warnings. In the backdrop of much dire reportage, the perception of Caucasian slavery intertwined with evolving religious and ideological paradigms. Clergymen, standing before their congregations, frequently invoked the plight of the captives, not merely as prayerful supplication but as sermonized condemnation of moral decay and societal complacency. "Shall we," they'd cry, "abandon our kin to heathen cruelty?" This rallying cry beckoned not only financial aid but beckoned moral rectitude.

Indeed, such media and public perception structured not just the ephemeral sentiments of the time but constructed a groundwork upon which policies, artistic expressions, and societal norms were built. Operating within this framework of emotional pertinacity, successive generations in the Enlightenment and after would recapitulate these perceptions, amalgamating them with contemporary understandings of liberty, virtue, and European identity.

Thus, the ink of yore, now yellowed with age, remains indelibly bracketed in the annals of European history. The public's perception, multifaceted and oftentimes contradictory, elucidated a demographic soul caught betwixt fear and fascination. The media, primitive by today's standards yet unyielding in its influence, shaped a collective memory that crossed borders and epochs. The gravity of this influence cannot be understated, for it reveals not just a reflection of societal attitudes and anxieties but also a potent instrument of historical continuity and transformation.

Chapter 7: The Legacy of Caucasian Slavery

The echo of Caucasian slavery resounds through the annals of history, a shadow casting its pallor over both Europe and the Ottoman Empire. This tragic legacy, inscribed not only in cultural memory but also etched into the genetic tapestry, serves as an indelible stain upon the conscience of these civilizations. As one gazes upon the long-term ramifications, the psychological and socio-economic scars stand out starkly, marooning entire populations in an intricate web of inherited trauma and systemic inequities. Contemporary historical narratives often grapple with this somber chronicle, sifting through the ashes of oppression to understand the far-reaching consequences. The narrative threads of Caucasian slavery continue to weave their way into the modern discourse, challenging our perceptions and compelling us to reevaluate the purported progress of human dignity and freedom.

Long-Term Effects on Europe and the Ottoman Empire

The legacy of Caucasian slavery woven into the intricate tapestry of European and Ottoman histories casts a haunting shadow that endures through centuries. Both realms, bound by the chains of human trade, witnessed a profound transformation, a metamorphosis fraught with sorrow and upheaval. In Europe, the ceaseless raids and the haunting specter of abductions instilled a collective paranoia, altering societal structures and diplomatic ties. Communities ravaged by loss were compelled to fortify their defenses, thus fostering a climate of perpetual vigilance. Meanwhile, the Ottoman Empire's reliance on an ocean of enslaved souls ensnared it in a web of moral and economic complexity. The ramifications of such dependency enfeebled local economies, skewing labor dynamics and instigating a cultural amalgamation that left indelible scars upon its social fabric. The bifurcation of these two civilizations, one as the perennial captor and the other the beleaguered victim, elucidates a dark chapter of mutual entanglement that can't be washed away by the relentless tides of time.

Cultural and Genetic Impact is a sub-section that unveils a profound chapter in the annals of human suffering and resilience, particularly as it pertains to the plight of Caucasian slaves in the Ottoman Empire. The ripple effects of this era have etched themselves deeply into the cultural and genetic fabric of the regions involved, weaving a complex tapestry whose threads of memory and identity stretch across centuries.

The cultural impact of Caucasian slavery in the Ottoman Empire is palpable even today. The forced integration of slaves into Ottoman society led to an uneasy blending of cultures. This created a melting pot of traditions, languages, and practices. Enslaved Europeans, often from Italy, Spain, and other Mediterranean regions, brought with them their customs and religions. The Ottoman Empire, already a mosaic of diverse peoples, absorbed these new elements, albeit through the lens of domination and subjugation.

One of the most visible impacts is seen in the architecture and urban planning of former Ottoman territories. Churches, schools, and homes built by enslaved Europeans still stand, bearing witness to their skill and craftsmanship. These structures, often built under duress, now serve as silent reminders of the past. Simultaneously, the adoption and adaptation of European styles into local designs can be observed in various historical edifices throughout the Ottoman Empire's expanse.

The genetic impact of the Caucasian slavery period cannot be overstated. The blending of populations led to significant genetic intermingling. Over generations, many descendants of slaves and their Ottoman captors formed new ethnic and genetic identities. This genetic infusion has enriched the gene pool of the regions involved, but it also carries the scars of forced unions and disrupted lives.

While some European captives were integrated into the Ottoman family structures, many others were subjected to roles that eroded their sense of identity and belonging. Female slaves, in particular, often found themselves in the Sultan's harems, where they bore children who would go on to play significant roles in the empire's lore. These children of mixed heritage sometimes rose to prominent positions within the Ottoman administration, their lineage a blend of European bloodlines and Ottoman authority.

The infusion of European genes into the Ottoman population was not merely a passive occurrence but also a calculated strategy by the empire. Marriages and procreation were often encouraged, not for the sake of unity, but to strengthen the empire's genetic and social structure. The offspring of such unions stood as living bridges between cultures, carrying the legacies of both their European and Ottoman heritage.

Language serves as another testament to this blending. The colloquial speech in many parts of the former Ottoman territories still contains traces of European influences brought by the slaves. Words, phrases, and even grammatical structures that were absorbed into the local languages have persisted through the ages. These linguistic artifacts are whispers of a past where cultures clashed and coalesced under the yoke of oppression.

Traditional music and folktales, too, were profoundly impacted by this period of slavery. The sorrowful songs that narrate tales of longing and loss, as well as the cautionary tales that recount the horrors of capture and servitude, echo through the generations. They are not just stories but collective memories, encoded in the rhythms and melodies passed down through the years.

Religious syncretism is another facet of the cultural impact. Many European slaves who were Christians found themselves practicing their faith in secret or blending it with Islam, the dominant religion in the Ottoman Empire. This necessity to hide or syncretize their religious practices led to intriguing fusions of belief systems. Over time, these evolved into unique religious traditions that carried elements of both Christianity and Islam, reflecting the forced integration of the slave populations.

The psychological impact on the descendants of these slaves is nuanced and profound. The generational trauma of captivity, forced assimilation, and identity loss lingers in the collective consciousness of these communities. Historical memory, filtered through stories told by ancestors, carries an undercurrent of fear and resilience, shaping how these descendants perceive their place in the world.

In some regions, the legacy of Caucasian slavery has given rise to a dual sense of identity. Descendants of slaves might identify with both their European and Ottoman heritage, creating a complex self-conception that navigates between pride and pain. This dual identity often manifests in unique cultural practices, dietary traditions, and social norms that echo the blending of two vastly different worlds under the shadow of enslavement.

The arts, particularly literature and visual arts, also reflect the cultural impact of this slave history. Many works of art created in the aftermath of this period grapple with themes of captivity, freedom, and the search for identity. These artistic expressions serve as both a cathartic exercise for the creators and a poignant reminder for future generations of the dark chapters their ancestors endured.

One particularly striking example can be found in the epic narratives and poems that have survived from the era. Poets and bards, many of whom were themselves descendants of slaves, wove intricate tales of heroism and tragedy that encapsulated the emotional and physical struggles of their forebears. These literary works are invaluable historical documents that provide insight into the lived experiences of those bound by the chains of slavery.

Institutionally, the legacy of Caucasian slavery has left an indelible mark on the administrative and military structures of the former Ottoman territories. Many descendants of slaves integrated into the military and governmental ranks, their unique heritage influencing policy and strategy. Their contributions, often overlooked, are crucial to understanding the development of these institutions.

Moreover, the economic impact of Caucasian slavery, from the labor provided to the markets driven by the trade, has shaped the socio-economic trajectories of the regions involved. The prosperity built on the backs of slaves has trickled down through generations, impacting wealth distribution and social stratification in ways that are often unacknowledged but deeply ingrained.

In conclusion, the cultural and genetic impacts of Caucasian slavery within the Ottoman Empire are intricate and far-reaching. They are woven into the very fabric of the societies that were touched by this dark period of human history. The legacy of this era, marked by forced cultural exchange and genetic melding, serves as a powerful reminder of the enduring human capacity for resilience and adaptation in the face of profound adversity. The echoes of this past continue to resonate in the cultural practices, genetic heritage, and collective memories of the present, inviting an ongoing dialogue about identity, history, and the complex interplay of oppression and survival.

Modern Historical Narratives

The tale of Caucasian slavery, much like the shadowy corridors of an ancient fortress, has left its indelible marks on the annals of history. In the realm of modern historical narratives, the echoes of these chains persist, a constant reminder of a past society would rather forget. Today's historical discourse often finds itself entrapped between the sepia-tinged lore of yesteryears and the cold, hard facts demanded by scholarly rigor.

Modern historical narratives about Caucasian slavery strive to paint an accurate picture, one that strips away the romanticized veneer and allows the stark reality to be laid bare. Ever since the waning days of the Ottoman Empire, historians have grappled with the task of disentangling these stories from the biased viewpoints of contemporary chroniclers. The role of Barbary pirates and the deep-seated economic dependencies of the time are aspects that today's narratives endeavor to elucidate, ensuring that the interpretation of primary sources remains faithful to the lived experiences of those enslaved.

The transformation of these narratives over time reflects a shift in how societies choose to remember their pasts. During the early days of European historiography, the grim tale of Caucasian slavery often was diluted with noble tales of resistance and rebellion, glossing over the day-to-day struggles of the enslaved. Modern narratives, however, delve deeper. They recount the harrowing raids, the relentless capture, the squalid conditions on slave ships, and the brutal life of forced labor in alien lands. These stark depictions serve to remind contemporary audiences of the depths of human suffering and resilience.

Integrating these narratives into the broader tapestry of world history challenges modern historians to navigate a labyrinth of moral and ethical quandaries. Distinguishing myth from reality requires painstaking research, critical analysis, and, above all, a commitment to truth. Contemporary scholars labor to separate the romanticized accounts of adventurers and explorers from the harrowing realities faced by the enslaved. Far from being relegated to the margins of historical discourse, the plight of Caucasian slaves now occupies a central position in discussions about human rights and systemic oppression.

One of the principal challenges in constructing these narratives lies in addressing the myriad social issues that cloud public perception. Historians must confront deeply ingrained prejudices and misconceptions, often stemming from long-standing cultural biases. The myth of the "white slave" as an oxymoron pervades popular culture, obfuscating the lived reality of those who endured such suffering. Through nuanced storytelling, historians strive to dismantle these stereotypes, providing a platform for a more inclusive and accurate representation of the past.

Moreover, the modern discourse around Caucasian slavery brings to the fore questions of cultural identity and memory. The long-term effects on both Europe and the Ottoman Empire have been profound, influencing cultural and genetic legacies that persist to this day. In weaving these threads into contemporary historical narratives, scholars reveal the enduring interconnectedness of past and present, challenging communities to reconcile with the haunting specters of their shared histories.

The implications of these narratives extend beyond academia, influencing public policy and education. Addressing the gaps in historical knowledge necessitates a concerted effort to incorporate these stories into curricula, ensuring future generations understand the complexities of their heritage. Media representation also plays a crucial role in shaping public perception. As historians, we bear the responsibility of guiding this portrayal, advocating for a portrayal that respects the gravity of the subject matter without sensationalizing the suffering of those who endured it.

Offsetting contemporary social amnesia involves engaging with historical revisionism and its consequences. Modern narratives serve as a bulwark against the erasure of uncomfortable truths, ensuring that the stories of Caucasian slaves are preserved with the dignity and respect they deserve. This requires a delicate balance—embracing the Gothic and macabre elements of their experience without losing sight of the humanity at the heart of these tales.

As we reflect on the evolution of these narratives, we glimpse the broader arc of historical storytelling. From early accounts that merely brushed the surface to contemporary works that unearth deeper truths, the journey of understanding Caucasian slavery demands continual reexamination and reinterpretation. The shadow of the past is long, but the light of scholarly inquiry can penetrate even its darkest corners.

Ultimately, modern historical narratives about Caucasian slavery serve a dual purpose. They honor the memory of those who suffered and forge a path for contemporary society to learn from past transgressions. By embracing the lessons of history, we can address present-day injustices and strive toward a more equitable future. The saga of Caucasian slavery, enshrined in the annals of historical discourse, stands as both a cautionary tale and a beacon of resilience.

Chapter 8: Comparison with African Slavery

In a macabre tableau of human suffering, one must juxtapose the plight of Caucasian slaves against that of their African counterparts to discern the variances and gravities of their agonies. Across the oppressors' spectrums, the Ottoman Empire's shadows enveloped the Caucasian thralls, their spirits subjugated under a different light but similar chains as those that bound the souls ferried across the Atlantic. Yet, the stark contrasts in treatment, labor, and roles within their respective realms cast a cri de coeur, an echo of injustice defined not merely by geography but by the intrinsic inequities borne upon the flesh and sinew of these oppressed. While African slaves toiled agonizingly in plantations and were oft rendered disposable, Caucasian slaves found themselves woven into the Ottoman societal fabric—used for both menial labors and specialized crafts but rendered equally voiceless. This symbiotic cruelty catalyzed distinct economic and cultural ramifications, etching disparate yet interconnected legacies upon the annals of history. In statistical shadows, one finds the quantitative horror, yet it's within the human narratives that the true essence of suffering across these disparate yet parallel corridors of bondage revealed itself in gripping melancholia.

Key Differences in Treatment and Labor

The distinction between the treatment and labor of Caucasian slaves in the Ottoman Empire and that of African slaves in various other contexts weaves a dark, intricate tapestry of human suffering, contrasting sharply in several aspects. Caucasian slaves, often seized by Barbary pirates, endured a spectrum of fates; some were shackled to brutal manual labor in the sprawling fields and suffocating mines, while others found themselves in more 'privileged' positions, enslaved within opulent households, serving under masters who held the power of life and death over them. These slaves, uprooted from their homeland, were thrust into a world where their worth was measured solely by their utility and subservience. Though both African and Caucasian slaves experienced unimaginable torment, the Ottoman approach to slavery was less about the color of one's skin and more an unrelenting pursuit of economic and social dominance. This multifaceted cruelty, punctuated by severe punishments and layered social hierarchies, underscored the relentless endeavor to maintain control, breaking bodies and spirits to sustain an empire built on human misery.

Specific Roles Blended into Ottoman Empire Elegance cloaked in chain and dire sorrow infused with pomp, the enigma of Caucasian slaves in the Ottoman Empire unveils itself in intricate layers. The symbiotic relationship between the captives and their captors forged a peculiar blend of roles that defy conventional historical narratives. These roles, seamlessly woven into the tapestry of Ottoman society, were as diverse as the myriad cultures entangled within the Empire's sprawling dominion.

From the stark desolate quarters of newly seized captives to the ornate halls where some rose to prominence, the integration of Caucasian slaves into the Ottoman Empire defies simplistic definitions. Here, hierarchy didn't strictly dictate roles as one might anticipate. Instead, individuals found themselves cast in positions as varied as the Empire's geography. Passing from servitude to positions of considerable influence, some Caucasian slaves navigated an existence oscillating between bondage and authority.

Consider the devshirme system, a stark embodiment of this blend. Christian boys, snatched from their homelands, were converted to Islam and drafted into the Imperial workforce. The sultan's selection process was both a curse and a peculiar form of elevation. Thus transformed, these young souls often ascended to military or administrative prominence, their loyalty first to the Ottoman throne. The Janissaries, an elite military corps, were perhaps the most renowned manifestation of this odious yet upward mobility. For all the terror of their abduction, their toil wielded a paradoxical power within the Sultan's grand designs.

In urban centers, the presence of Caucasian slaves extended beyond the barracks and palaces. Scholars note their vitality in artisan trades and domestic service, providing indispensable support to the polygynous Ottoman households. These urban slaves, unlike their rural counterparts, often experienced a degree of cultural and social fusion. In some instances, they acquired elevated status and influenced local customs, subtly yet inexorably leaving their mark on Ottoman urban life.

The rural landscape painted a grimmer portrait. Here, Caucasian slaves toiled under harsher conditions, bound to the soil much like their sub-

Saharan counterparts. Yet, their interactions with Ottoman rural life created a mosaic of cultural and agricultural hybridity. The transference of agricultural techniques and culinary customs from the Caucasus to the Anatolian plains is a testament to this fusion, an eloquent yet tragic narrative of cultural exchange under duress.

Particularly intriguing are the eunuchs, whose lives encapsulate a spectrum of power and vulnerability. Often sourced from Circassian and Georgian slaves, these men were castrated and relegated to serve within the intimate confines of the harem. Here, the blend of rigid roles and unexpected influence reached its zenith. Eunuchs wielded considerable control within the harem, managing its intricate hierarchy and occasionally advising the Sultan and his court. The potency of their position serves as a stark reminder of the convoluted dynamics at play.

Among the most notable of these eunuchs was Beshir Agha, who, despite his initial chains, rose to unprecedented eminence within the palace's sheltered walls. His story, replete with irony and intrigue, symbolizes the often contradictory existence of such figures who straddled the line between servitude and sovereignty. The harem, under his watchful gaze, became a stage where power dynamics unfurled in whispers and shadows.

The edukated amongst these slaves adorned the Ottoman court with their erudition, becoming pivotal in diplomacy and statesmanship. They served as translators, diplomats, and secretaries, their proficiency in multiple languages an asset in the Empire's vast and varied territories. Their presence reflected a confluence of cultures, an intermingling of traditions that, while enforced, enriched the administrative machinery of the Ottoman state.

The religious transformation imposed upon Caucasian slaves adds another layer to their intricate roles. Forced conversions to Islam were not mere acts of subjugation but of assimilation and, occasionally, of elevation. These converted individuals often rose within the military and administrative ranks, their new faith a bridge to Ottoman inner machinations. The conversion narrative is emblematic of the intricate amalgamation of coercion and opportunity, a duality etched into the lives of those who walked the Sultan's halls.

The attention afforded to female slaves reveals yet another dimension of this complex integration. While many endured the agonies of servitude, distinct fates awaited those who captivated the Sultan's fancy. Elevated to positions within the imperial harem, these women influenced courtly politics and, through their offspring, the very succession of the throne. Roxelana, born as a Ruthenian slave, illustrates this tale. Her rise to become Süleyman the Magnificent's favorite wife changed the course of Ottoman history.

These women, entrapped in gilded cages, wielded power shrouded in intimacy and intrigue. They fostered alliances, counseled the Sultan, and occasionally orchestrated political maneuvers that reverberated beyond the harem's confines. Their stories, blurred by legend and history, encapsulate the paradox of empowerment amid oppression.

The roles of Caucasian slaves, thus, can't be neatly categorized. Blended into the Ottoman Empire's fabric, their plights and positions reflected the complex and often contradictory nature of the Empire itself. From warriors to scholars, administrators to concubines, they were threads in a grand, albeit tragic, tapestry of historical convergence and cultural amalgamation.

While discussing the multifaceted roles of Caucasian slaves within the Ottoman Empire, one cannot ignore the undercurrents of resistance and adaptation. These individuals, despite their bondage, strained against their chains in myriad ways, defying a simplistic narrative of submission. Their contributions, often coerced, have left an indelible mark on the cultural and administrative legacy of the Ottoman Empire.

Thus, the odyssey of Caucasian slaves in the Ottoman fold is one etched in blood and ambition, sorrow and hope. It is a somber reminder of humanity's capacity for both cruelty and resilience, a testament to the enduring spirit of those who, though shackled, influenced an empire's destiny. Their roles, woven with paradox and poignance, extend beyond mere servitude, offering a profound glimpse into the intricate mosaic of history.

Statistical Comparisons

In examining the statistical mechanics underlying the grim phenomenon of Caucasian slavery in the Ottoman Empire, one cannot help but draw stark contrasts with the numerics encapsulating African slavery. The comparison illuminates a tapestry woven with figures that tell tales of a different ilk yet echo a strangely familiar woe. The sheer volume of African slaves far exceeds that of Caucasian captives, a fact that gnaws persistently at the historical conscience.

Between the 16th and 19th centuries, estimates suggest that approximately one million to one and a half million Europeans fell prey to the clutches of Barbary slavery. This number pales when juxtaposed with the horrendous magnitude of the transatlantic slave trade, which saw an estimated twelve to thirteen million Africans brutally transported across the Atlantic to the Americas. This yawning chasm in scales is profound, yet it belies the suffering uncaptured by mere frequencies.

Nonetheless, the comparative impacts of these slave trades can't solely be measured by raw quantities. The demographic shifts and societal upheavals resulting from these trades require deeper scrutiny. Demographically, the capture of Caucasian slaves largely affected coastal regions of Europe, devastating small towns and coastal villages through relentless raids by the Barbary corsairs. The impact, while geographically focused, still inflicted widespread societal disruption.

On the other hand, the African slave trade saw entire populated regions of the African continent being systematically depleted of their human resources. In areas like Senegambia, West Central Africa, and the Bight of Benin, the slaver's shadow stretched far and wide. The displacement of able-bodied men and women, integral to communal and familial structures, restructured societies to an unrecognizable extent. The deleterious effects included not just a demographic imbalance but also a generational disruption that echoes through the centuries.

One cannot ignore the comparative mortality rates within these trade systems. Caucasian captives, particularly in the early stages of capture and transportation, were subjected to abysmal survival conditions. Frigid holds of ships, poor nutrition, and unspeakable sanitation standards led to high mortality rates. Studies suggest a mortality rate ranging from 10% to as high as 20% during the sea voyage and the initial months of captivity. Similar or even higher mortality rates afflicted African slaves in the Middle Passage, where cramped quarters, inadequate supplies, and ruthless enforcement of order resulted in catastrophic death tolls.

Another statistical layer worth examining is the gender distribution among these captives. The records indicate a significant tilt towards male captives in both slave trades, albeit for different purposes. In the Ottoman context, males were predominantly sought for their labor utility and military potential, being pressed into service as galley slaves, agricultural laborers, or janissaries. Meanwhile, the transatlantic trade saw males prized for their hard labor potential on plantations and in mines, though women, too, were captured in vast numbers.

An intriguing comparison arises when examining the period of servitude before manumission or death. For Ottoman Caucasian slaves, there existed a—though seldom walked—path to social mobility. Conversion to Islam could sometimes, albeit rarely, facilitate a transition from servitude to a semblance of freedom and even integration into Ottoman society. Some captives, through military or administrative service, achieved positions of moderate influence and autonomy. Contrastingly, African slaves in the Americas faced a near-perpetual bondage with few avenues towards freedom, completely at the mercy of their masters. Even freedmen (those rare African slaves who gained manumission) faced entrenched systemic barriers preventing any real assimilation into the broader society.

Wages, revenues, and economic yields also present divergent narratives in the statistical comparison of these two types of slavery. In the Ottoman markets, the price tags attached to Caucasian captives were significantly influenced by factors like age, gender, skills, and even appearance. Young, handsome boys and beautiful girls fetched exorbitant prices, often entering lives of domestic servitude or worse, the harem. These captive markets in Algerian, Tunisian, and Libyan cities provided a substantial revenue stream that oiled the gears of Ottoman commerce.

In the Americas, African slaves were the lifeblood of an agrarian economy dependent on the output of colossal plantations. This institutional economic model engendered a highly transactional view of human life, where slave labor drove the massive production scales of crops like sugar, cotton, and tobacco. The market dynamics here were no less brutal; the value of slaves was appraised based on their labor capacity, demarcating men for heavy labor and women for both servitude and reproduction purposes, to perpetuate the labor force.

To delve deeper, the workforce composition in these two types of slavery offers an enlightening statistical veneer. In the Ottoman territory, slaves fulfilling military roles or those coerced into skilled labor were in sharper focus. It is estimated that a significant proportion of Caucasian slaves found themselves in the administration, battling roles as court retainers or in some instances, ascending to the status of eunuchs in the harem hierarchy. However, a sizable chunk of this populace, perhaps around 60%, was engaged in agrarian or domestic labor—a clear distinction from the predominantly plantation-focused toil of African slaves.

Within the murky depths of these statistics, another layer unravels—the patterns of resistance and escape. For Caucasian slaves, the proximity to Europe offered a ghostly glimmer of hope. Escapes often involved covertly reaching European ships docked along Mediterranean coasts. Conversely, the African slaves' aspirations for freedom led to maroon communities, quilombos, and larger organized revolts like Nat Turner's rebellion. Although differing in magnitude, both groups cyclically sparked resistance movements, a testament to the indomitable human spirit clawing for emancipation.

The socioeconomic repercussions on the captured populations' homelands were both immediate and long-lasting. For Europe, the lingering dread of pirate raids fostered coastal fortifications, naval vigilance, and even instilled a cultural fear of the "Barbary Terror."

Contrastingly, African regions suffered a systemic disruption of social structures, political entities, and economic stability. The forced exodus of millions of Africans not only robbed communities of their most vital members but also sowed internal strife that would echo through subsequent tribal conflicts and colonial subjugation.

In parsing these numerical tales, historians aren't merely sifting through dry facts but are reconstructing the existential plights and the historically endured suffering of these forgotten faces. The intricate balance of statistics doesn't diminish the horror but invites us to comprehend its multifaceted reality. Indeed, numbers offer plain evidence and silent testimony, charting a path towards understanding that transcends the mere accumulation of data.

Chapter 9: Contemporary Discourse on Slavery

As modern observers, we find ourselves ensnared in a web of ignorance and apathy toward the historical plight of Caucasian slaves—a forgotten chapter often overshadowed by other narratives in the annals of human cruelty. This tragic oversight flourishes in the fertile soil of educational gaps and media misrepresentation, where the unrelenting tides of historical revisionism threaten to erode the harsh truths and stark realities endured by these forgotten souls. Within this labyrinth of misinformation, the pain and suffering endured by Caucasian slaves are diminished, distorted, or wholly erased, casting a dark and foreboding shadow over our collective historical consciousness. The persistence of this narrative not only silences the voices of the past but also reshapes our understanding of history, perpetuating a cycle of unawareness that undermines genuine efforts toward justice and reconciliation. Hence, the quest for historical accuracy becomes a battle against time itself, one wherein historians must wield the torch of truth to illuminate the obscured corridors of our shared past.

Modern Ignorance and Apathy

In this age of seeming enlightenment, a veil of ignorance and apathy has descended upon the annals of history, especially regarding Caucasian slaves. Modern narratives, plagued by selective amnesia, often neglect the harrowing ordeals endured by these individuals. Where the etchings of whips and chains should evoke empathy and remembrance, a chilling indifference reigns. Society's propensity to cast Caucasian slavery into the shadows, dismissing it as an irrelevant relic, only deepens this dark abyss of forgetfulness. This negligence not only skews the historical record but also perpetuates a cycle of ignorance, blinding contemporary discourse to the full spectrum of human subjugation and suffering. Apathy, thus, becomes a cruel shackle, binding the present to a distorted past, and historians must labor against this tide to illuminate truth's forgotten corridors.

Educational Gaps and Media Representation stagger and veil the truths of Caucasian slavery, casting shadows upon textured history's full disclosure. A spectral aura envelopes the lessons oft untaught, as classroom dialogues imbibe fragments—an incomplete mosaic. Forgotten are the narratives of those who toiled under Ottoman suns, their stories dimmed by the vibrant retelling of more widely known slaveries. Why does the pedagogic gaze avert so?

In education systems across the Euro-American world, the brutal captivity of Caucasians by the Barbary Pirates—a narrative etched into accounts of the Ottoman Empire—remains woefully underexposed. History curricula seldom lend credence to the suffering and struggles of these subjugates. One finds textbooks laconic, perhaps deliberately so, on this dark chapter. Whereas Transatlantic slavery burgeons with visibility, a scholarly void persists for Caucasians enslaved along Mediterranean coasts. This void is not merely an academic oversight but a calculated omission that sustains bias in historical understanding.

Ah, but the chasm in knowledge does not pervade academia alone. The media, both historical and contemporary, plays the accomplice in this grand omission. Glance through screenplays, historical novels, or mass media coverage, and the discerning eye finds scant mention of Caucasian slaves, let alone a balanced portrayal. When the Barbary captivities do breach the fortress of popular narratives, they are often shrouded in exoticism, relegated to sidelines, or their significance diluted—mere footnotes in the grandiloquent annals of history.

Consider the narratives spun by cinema and television: these are the contemporary griots, shaping public perception with moving images and seductive storylines; however, rarely do these narratives pay homage to the plight of European captives in North Africa. Imagine a world where every tale of suffering and survival by Caucasians in captivity was visualized with the same vigor and regularity as those harrowing voyages across the Atlantic. The cognitive dissonance borne from such omissions distorts collective memory, perpetuating a skewed historical consciousness.

Indeed, the very fabric of contemporary society's understanding of historic and systemic bondage is compromised by these omissions. An interesting dichotomy arises within the dichotomy itself: the Barbary captives are both remembered and erased, their histories expounded in academic circles yet cloaked from the broader public's awareness. The deliberate or inadvertent exclusion of Caucasian slavery from the curriculum and media narratives echoes with Socratic disquiet—a sense of knowledge half-attained, truth half-told.

The ramifications of these educational voids ripple through time, affecting perceptions and policy. People are more likely to empathize with what they know, what they have been taught to see. When the torment and resistance of Caucasian captives remain concealed behind a veil, it narrows the avenues for comprehensive empathy. The significance of historic slavery becomes pigeonholed, a one-dimensional view that neglects the full array of human suffering. And thus, our societal dialogues, our reconciliations and redistributions, wear a form of bias so ingrained that it passes often without question.

The media's presentation of slavery, when juxtaposed against educational gaps, acts on the public psyche like water on stone, shaping and wearing down the contours of collective memory. The narratives consumed daily influence how slavery's legacy is perceived and understood. This is not merely a case of underrepresentation or poor coverage; it is a poetic injustice to the spirits whose screams were stifled by the Barbary wind. A media landscape that continuously ignores or glosses over the Caucasian experience of slavery fosters an incomplete moral reckoning. Through such media silence, one implicitly condones a fragmented historical perspective that hinders modern reparative discourses.

Moreover, the absence of these narratives in educational curricula implies a tacit censoring of history's multiplicity. Students graduate with a blinkered view, a truncated understanding of servitude that fails to encompass the comprehensive human ordeal. How might the discourse change if educational frameworks embraced and elucidated the full spectrum of slavery, including the Caucasians in Ottoman dominion? The repercussions would cut across disciplines, engendering more nuanced discussion around historic injustices and their remnants in today's society. The benefits of such an inclusive curriculum would be manifold: a richer, more empathetic understanding of human history, and a more robust appreciation of resilience.

In this clash between what is taught and what is shown, lies an arena for historians to wield their pens like daggers, slicing through the veils of ignorance. The task falls upon the chroniclers and guardians of memory to present an unvarnished narrative—to fill these educational voids and to demand from media a portrayal as rich and varied as history itself.

When we unearth these buried tales, shine light upon the dark chapters rather than romanticize or overshadow them, we don a mantle of responsibility—a responsibility to the truth, to a heritage that for too long has suffered dormancy beneath academia's cold stones and media's evanescent tides. Historians, then, are charged with an unending quest: to restore coherence to a fragmented narrative, knitting together the disparate threads of human suffering into a comprehensive, albeit somber tapestry.

In sum, the interplay between educational gaps and media representation of Caucasian slavery is no benign misstep; it is a grievous hole in the fabric of collective memory. Calibrating this balance, ensuring these shadows are cast away, calls for a dedicated scholarly pursuit, a relentless digging into archives and a vociferous demand for balanced portrayals. Only then can we hope to achieve not merely an accurate, but a truthful reckoning with historical reality, thus fostering an informed and empathetic society.

Historical Revisionism and Its Consequences

In the labyrinthine corridors of contemporary discourse on slavery, echoes of past injustices reverberate more potently than ever, urging us to examine not only what was but also what could have been. The sepulchral shadows of historical revisionism often glide unnoticed, yet their insidious presence has the power to alter collective memory, distorting the scarred visage of Caucasian slavery into something unrecognizable— and therein lies the peril.

Historical revisionism, the deliberate act of reinterpreting the past to serve present agendas, wields a double-edged sword. On one side, it serves as a tool for uncovering long-muted voices. On the other, it risks obfuscating the poignantly dire narratives of Caucasian slaves under the Ottoman yoke. Those who engage in this recalibration often tread on fragile grounds, where the delicate filaments of fact and fiction intertwine. This careful dance can lead either to enlightenment or to egregious misapprehensions that seek to placate modern sensibilities, neglecting the raw verity of historical suffering.

The obsession with smoothing the jagged edges of history manifests itself in various forms, each with its dire consequences. Official textbooks may subtly omit the mention of ferocious Barbary raids or the abject conditions endured by captives. This seemingly benign omission results in generations growing up bereft of genuine historical knowledge. "What you do not see," they say, "cannot hurt you," but in truth, what is unseen festers in the recesses of collective ignorance, creating a chasm dark and deep.

Revisionism, in its most malevolent guise, conspires to rewrite the annals of agony. It portrays slaves not as wretched beings shackled in an alien land, but as willing participants in some grand societal tableau, contributing voluntarily to the Ottoman Empire's prosperity. Such narratives all but erase the rust-tinged chains and the ceaseless labor under a punishing sun, leaving behind a polished veneer which historians must diligently scrape away to reveal the raw substance of the past.

One cannot ignore the contemporary backlash against the accurate retelling of history. Efforts to cast a scrutinizing light on the Caucasian slaves' plight often collide with the impermeable walls of political correctness. In this era where public discourse is fashioned by media portrayal, the hard truths about historical slavery are traded for more palatable fictions. This dilution of historical narratives doesn't merely obscure the past—it unfurls pernicious ripples across academic and public spheres.

The ripple effects of this distortion are multifold, as historical revisionism creeps into policy-making and educational outreach. In academia, where the pursuit of truth should reign supreme, revisionists wield influence like court jesters who whisper into the ears of kings. Their reconciliation of painful histories with more sanguine tales manages to seep into scholarly articles, conferences, and curriculum. Young minds, desperate for clarity and comprehension, are instead fed spoonfuls of saccharine, bereft of the bitterness that true history demands.

Further, the consequences extend beyond academia into the very fabric of contemporary social interactions. The romanticized notion of the "noble enslaved" infiltrates societies' understanding of past injustices. This troubling image negates the domestic and international resistance movements that arose to contest the brutal reality. It's not just a crime against memory; it's an erasure of valiant struggles, the untold sagas of those who dared to rise against their shackles.

In conversations over reparative measures and memorials, historical revisionism offers a perilous counter-narrative. It dilutes the impetus for genuine acts of remembrance, positioning these injustices as historical footnotes rather than foundational sins requiring redress. This ideological shift creates vacuums where robust discussions about reparations and historical reconciliations should occur. Indeed, the revisionist approach can also result in skewed public sentiments and a misguided sense of historical equity.

Public perception, invariably molded by revisionist history, shapes collective consciousness. Cultural products—films, books, even social media narratives—begin to reflect and perpetuate these inaccuracies. Such reflections do more than entertain; they indoctrinate. The inaccurate portrayal of Caucasian slavery in popular media anchors these misconceptions in the public psyche, thereby perpetuating a sanitized version of the past that is easier to digest but wholly unrepresentative of the anguish experienced by the enslaved.

The consequences of historical revisionism are not confined merely to distorted academic discourses or compromised cultural memories. They also palpably affect contemporary social and political landscapes. Misinformed civic debates hinge upon these rewritten histories, shaping ill-conceived policies and fostering societal rifts. Discussions on race, equity, and justice become marred by a foundational inaccuracy— conversations that should inspire healing and unity are sullied by the toxic effluvium of misrepresented truths.

To counteract these treacherous repercussions, historians bear the weighty mantle of truth. It is incumbent upon them to fight against the tides of revisionism, to ensure that future generations inherit an unblemished chronicle of human suffering and resilience. Indeed, the role of historians extends beyond mere recording; they must act as sentinels who guard against the encroachment of falsehoods. These guardians of truth must actively engage in public discourse, correct inaccuracies, and advocate for a history unvarnished by contemporary expediencies.

A collective effort must emerge to unmask these corrosive revisions. This involves not merely painstaking archival work but also the dissemination of true narratives through diverse platforms—academic journals, public lectures, mainstream media, and digital domains. Educational systems must be recalibrated to include accurate portrayals of Caucasian slavery, incorporating the raw, harrowing details that historical revisionism seeks to obscure.

Every unveiling of truth, however small, represents a victory against the forces intent on burying it. The wounds of our collective past, when aired in their full, gruesome authenticity, provide fertile ground for genuine understanding and reconciliation. The sacrifices and sufferings of Caucasian slaves under the Ottoman Empire must, therefore, be immortalized in their full, painful glory—not sanitized for modern consumption but revered as testaments to human endurance and the indomitable quest for freedom.

In conclusion, the encroachment of historical revisionism within the framework of Caucasian slavery brings forth consequences as dark and insidious as the practice it seeks to reframe. It is a theft of truth and an affront to the memory of the fallen. Historians, as the sentinels of the past, must rise against this tide, ensuring that the unadulterated truth stands unchallenged as a beacon for future generations. The ghosts of the past, shrouded in the tattered veils of history, demand nothing less.

Chapter 10: Addressing Historical Injustices

Amidst the convoluted tapestry of bygone epochs, the shadows of historical injustices loom large, casting long, indelible marks upon the present. The harrowing plight of Caucasian slaves, often mired in obscurity, demands redress not merely through spoken contrition but via tangible reparative measures and commemorative memorials. These gestures, intrinsically woven into the fabric of societal rectitude, strive to assuage the wounds inflicted by centuries of oppression. Encountering myriad efforts—engendered by nations, communities, and solitary advocates—one discerns tales of both resplendent success and disheartening stagnation. Yet, therein lies the path to collective healing: embracing truth, fostering understanding, and charting a course that emboldens us to move beyond the vestiges of suffering into realms of solace and reconciliation.

Reparative Measures and Memorials

The annals of time, heavy with sorrowful tales of Caucasian slaves, beckon us to contemplate the grave reparations needed to atone for such historical atrocities. With a heart laden in gravitas, one must acknowledge that mere recognition falls short of true justice. Across the continents lie echoes of their unheard cries, demanding tributes both tangible and intangible. Statues and plaques, while visually poignant, are but stepping stones; the true reparative measures involve revamping educational curricula and fostering an enduring societal remembrance. Memorials should not just immortalize the anguish but also serve as harbingers of enlightenment, ensuring that future generations venerate the resilience of those who endured and tread carefully upon the ashes of their sacrifices. To cure the scars imprinted upon the collective soul, we must embrace a holistic approach melding historical veracity with contemporary restitution, thus creating a legacy that whispers tales of caution and resilience through the corridors of time.

Existing Efforts and Success Stories exist, illuminating the path toward a less egregious and fractured human history in which memory is salvaged and reparations are pursued. In the shadows of forgotten atrocities, diverse initiatives seek to acknowledge, memorialize, and rectify the history of Caucasian slavery with solemn determination. These endeavors, growing both from grassroots movements and authoritative bodies, unify in their quest to shed light on concealed chapters of oppression.

Organizations across the globe have pledged to spotlight the history of Caucasian slavery, drawing attention to its narratives and fostering acknowledgment in the public consciousness. Historical societies and academic institutions have erected memorials, funded research projects, and organized symposia to delve into these stories with the gravitas they demand. A notable example resides in the memorials erected in cities once known for their entanglement in the slave trade, forever marking the physical spaces where suffering unfolded.

Far and wide, cities from the European coastline to the heart of the Ottoman domain have begun to grapple earnestly with their haunted pasts. Museums dedicated to the bilateral narrative of the enslaved and enslavers have cropped up, transforming silent acknowledgments into active educational havens. For instance, the museum of slavery in Algiers contains relics and stories that encapsulate the harrowing experiences of Caucasian captives, promoting a broader understanding of this overlooked facet of history.

Literature, too, contributes to these efforts. Recent historical novels and scholarly publications recount the odysseys of stolen lives through vivid prose, blending factual recounting with poignant storytelling. These works ensure that the phantoms of the past gain voices potent enough to reach contemporary minds. They become rallying cries, enjoining readers not to turn a blind eye but to collectively mourn and learn.

Academics and historians have established coalitions to research and rectify the deficiencies in global historical education regarding Caucasian slavery. Historical conferences teem with papers and discussions focused on uncovering and disseminating these drowned-out stories. Notable among these efforts is the "Conference on Marginalized Histories," where scholars present works dedicated to revealing the intricacies and inhumanities borne by Caucasian slaves. By sharing these findings, they bridge gaping voids in historical record and fortify the collective memory against erasure.

Grassroots movements have arisen, advocating for formal apologies to be issued by states and institutions that benefited from or facilitated the trafficking of Caucasian lives. These platforms leverage the power of modern connectivity to rally support, disseminate information, and pressure governing bodies into action. Examples include the "Memoris of the Enslaved and Forgotten," an initiative that uses social media to gather stories and press for official acknowledgments and apologies. These campaigns, unflinching and insistent, draw attention to the need for both symbolic and tangible reparations.

In various countries, governments and local administrations have started to heed these calls, acknowledging their predecessors' complicity and expressing formal apologies. While these declarations cannot rectify the past, they signify steps toward a more ethically consistent and historically aware society. In some parts of Europe, these acknowledgments have been accompanied by educational reforms aimed at integrating the history of Caucasian slavery into primary and secondary curriculums, thereby ensuring future generations understand the full scope of their history.

Additional success stories emerge from international diplomatic efforts to address the historical wounds left by Caucasian slavery. Bilateral treaties between former trading nations now including clauses dedicated to the mutual recognition of past injustices and collaborative efforts to document historical narratives comprehensively. For example, the agreements between Turkey and several European nations include provisions for shared historical research projects and educational exchange programs centered on the history of slavery.

The role of non-governmental organizations proves indispensable in unearthing and memorializing the stories of those who endured Caucasian slavery. NGOs like "Voices Unseen" provide platforms for descendant communities to share their inherited trauma and cultural residue, thus enriching the global narrative with personal testimonies. Their work in excavating forgotten gravesites and preserving oral histories stands as a testament to the resilience of memory against the barrages of oblivion.

Restorative justice initiatives further complement these acknowledgments and memorials. Certain lineage-based support groups offer counseling to the descendants of victims, fostering a space for healing these intergenerational scars. Examples abound in programs that produce documentaries recounting the ordeal of the descendants who lost their ancestry and identity to the pervasive silence following their ancestors' enslavement.

Additionally, educational workshops and public lectures developed to enrich and influence contemporary perspectives on marginalized histories have risen in frequency and renown. These events offer insight into the complexities of Caucasian slavery, its socio-economic ripples, and its intercontinental consequences, thereby fostering a climate of reflection and learning.

Incorporating technology, digital archives and virtual reality projects enable anyone anywhere to interact with documented histories of Caucasian slavery. These innovative methods of historical engagement are being spearheaded by universities and historical societies, ensuring that remote audiences engage with challenging pasts in an immersive and impactful manner. Interactive maps, slave voyage databases, and virtual reconstructions of slave markets serve as modern-day textbooks, disturbing in their realism and invaluable in their educational capacity.

Parallel to these efforts stands the artistic representation of Caucasian slavery's legacy, portrayed through films, music, and visual arts. Films such as "Shadows of Chains" depict the raw and relentless experiences of captives, using cinema's power to etch these stories into the viewer's soul. Music, too, intertwines the somber notes of lost liberty with the triumphant strains of survival. Art installations in public spaces offer silent yet profound commentary on an otherwise overlooked history, challenging passersby to confront the nuanced grief and resilience of enslaved ancestors.

Finally, these collective efforts have, in part, led to policy changes aimed at compensating the descendants of those affected by Caucasian slavery. In rare but significant cases, former slave-owning institutions have established funds to support educational and economic opportunities for the progeny of those who suffered under their past actions. These reparative measures, while fledgling, signify a commitment to healing wounds that have stretched across the centuries.

Indeed, the work is extensive and ongoing, driven by a potent combination of acknowledgment, education, and reparation. It is only through these samplings of informed efforts—the lights in the darkened recesses of human history—that society can begin to reconcile and move forward. The legacy of Caucasian slavery, like any chapter of oppressed humanity, demands vigilance and remembrance, for only in facing the specters of our past do we ensure a future unmarred by the same calamitous mistakes. The efforts enumerated here serve as beacons, guiding us toward a more just and historically nuanced world.

Healing and Moving Forward

The winds of time, often merciless in their sweep, leave scars etched deep within the collective consciousness. Understanding the torment of those bound in chains is but the first step in a protracted journey. It is through the unrelenting pursuit of truth and the arduous task of reconciliation that the fabric of society may be mended, aligning history's errant threads towards a future where justice prevails.

In contemplating the path to healing and moving forward, one must peer into the hearts of both the aggrieved and the progeny of the oppressors. The crucible of human suffering, particularly that endured by Caucasian slaves within the Ottoman yoke, demands a multifaceted approach. Here, simple restitution will not suffice; there must be a deeper engagement, a cathartic reckoning with the past.

We might commence with memorials, somber yet profound in their intent. They serve as stark reminders, lest we forget the travails and tribulations of countless souls. Yet, memorials alone do little but whisper the names of the forgotten; they must be imbued with purpose, becoming sanctuaries for education and dialogue. Let these monuments transform into forums where descendants can engage with their history and pain, fostering a shared ethos of empathy.

Parallel to physical tributes, narrative reclamation assumes paramount importance. Academic platforms must be diligent in unearthing, preserving, and disseminating the stories of Caucasian slavery. Universities and historical societies ought to champion the inclusion of these narratives in curriculums, ensuring every generation acknowledges the full spectrum of human indignities wrought by the Ottoman Empire. Historians have a sacred duty here – they must wield their pens as swords, cutting through the obscurities and half-truths that veiled these injustices for too long.

Moreover, contemporary discourse needs to evolve beyond mere acknowledgement. The underpinnings of historical injustices must be critically analyzed to dismantle their lingering effects. Addressing the socio-economic and political legacies left in the wake of Ottoman slavery demands rigorous scholarship and public awareness campaigns. Governments and institutions, thus, carry the onus to fund and support initiatives aimed at redressing historical amnesia.

Diplomatic efforts, reminiscent of the treaties and ransoms once brokered to end slavery, should now forge new accords to aid nations and communities still reeling from this ancient scourge. Reparative measures can take myriad forms, from economic assistance to the restitution of cultural artifacts wrongfully appropriated during the eras of bondage.

Amidst these high-level efforts, grassroots movements bear equal significance. Community-driven reconciliation programs can catalyze understanding and healing at the local level. Workshops, discussion groups, and commemorative events foster communal solidarity and remind us that healing begins with individuals.

In the landscape of healing, art holds a mirror to society's soul. Artistic expression, in its myriad forms, offers a pathway to collective healing. The brushstrokes of a painter, the verses of a poet, and the melodies of a composer each weave a narrative that transcends scholarly discourse, engaging the heart in ways the mind alone cannot fathom. Public exhibitions and performances dedicated to portraying the anguish and resilience of those enslaved evoke a visceral empathy, bridging centuries-old divides.

Yet, moving forward also entails addressing the distortions and omissions that pervade our understanding of history. Historical revisionism, often wielded as a tool of denial or obfuscation, requires vigilant opposition. Ensuring academic rigor and integrity in the way we document and interpret the past is vital for authentic reconciliation.

Interwoven with these efforts must be a genuine commitment to inclusivity and diversity. The narratives of Caucasian slavery, juxtaposed with other historical injustices, enrich our understanding of humanity's complex tapestry of suffering and endurance. By fostering a holistic dialogue encompassing all oppressed groups, society can craft a more inclusive memory, thereby fostering mutual respect and unity.

- Education as a Cornerstone
- Community Engagement and Dialogue
- Art and Historical Memorials
- Evolving Discourse and Policy

Lastly, in weaving these threads together, we embrace a vision of history that does not merely recount past wrongs but also illuminates pathways to recompense and justice. As historians, our craft is not just to document but to bear witness, to become the custodians of a memory that serves as a beacon for a more just and compassionate world.

May this holistic approach in addressing the remnants of Caucasian slavery within the Ottoman Empire guide us toward true reconciliation, where the echoes of past afflictions become the harmonies of future concord.

Chapter 11: The Role of Historians in Shaping Memory

In the labyrinth of time, historians wield a formidable power, a blade that can carve through the veils of oblivion and reveal the spectral echoes of yesteryears. Their task bears an eerie nobility, one that binds them to the solemn duty of investigating, not only with unyielding rigor but also with a grave empathy for the silenced voices of Caucasian slaves. An immutable alliance with the truth demands they traverse ancient tomes and fading manuscripts, piecing together fractured tales, whilst their revelations ripple through academia in conferences and publications. Yet, their duty doesn't end at scholarly discourse. To truly forge the annals of collective memory, historians must descend from their scholarly towers, immersing themselves in public engagement, advocating with fervor in the ever-hazy present to illuminate the shadows of a neglected past. In doing so, they become the architects of memory, bending the erratic currents of historical consciousness towards a more enlightened and equitable understanding, freeing the past to inform a just future.

Investigating and Spreading Awareness

The solemn duty of historians transcends the mere recording of events; it is also to unearth obscured truths and lay bare the shadows that history would prefer forgotten. In addressing the plight of Caucasian slaves, we find ourselves not only explorers of the past but also torchbearers of justice, shedding light upon a neglected segment of human suffering. Through meticulous research and fervent dissemination, we must confront the specters of both indifference and ignorance that pervade contemporary discourse. By meticulously piecing together archival fragments and resurrecting the silenced voices, we arm ourselves with the formidable weapon of knowledge. Yet, this endeavor is not solitary; it entails a collective effort to transform academic findings into public consciousness. Through lectures, articles, and exhibitions, we must weave the dark tapestry of this history into the broader narrative, ensuring it captures the world's gaze and provokes reflection. In this investigative quest, our diligence becomes the catalyst for awareness, compelling society to reckon with its past and strive towards an enlightened future.

Academic Publications and Conferences serve as critical vessels in the intellectual odyssey that confronts the grim realities of Caucasian slavery in the Ottoman Empire, illuminating a past shrouded in shadows that many would prefer remain obscured. Such endeavors are not mere academic exercises; they are torches that pierce the darkness, illuminating truths with the potential to reshape collective consciousness. Scholarly works and interdisciplinary forums have, thus, become the linchpin in our understanding and dissemination of these harrowing chapters in history.

In the annals of scholarly pursuit, the academic publication akin to a whispering scribe holds an eminent place. Investigators and historians, steeped in erudition, have toiled through frightened nights and dim-lit libraries, sifting through a deluge of primary sources and esoteric records. Their diligent efforts culminate in works that serve both as robust narratives and repositories of empirical data. These texts unravel the complexities of Caucasian slavery, delineating the hierarchy of oppression within the Ottoman societal framework.

One cannot overlook the magnitude of journals dedicated to this ensnaring topic, wherein essayists unfurl the tapestries woven with threads of agony and resistance. These journals range from specialized periodicals centered on Ottoman history to broader publications that examine slavery in its multitudinous forms. The intricate net of citations within these texts binds them to the eternal fabric of historical discourse, connecting the threads of individual stories to the grander canvas of human suffering and resilience.

Amongst the cavalcade of academic work, certain seminal publications have made indelible marks. Monographs and anthologies capture the gamut—from the initial raids and heart-wrenching transport of captured souls to their grueling lives as forced laborers in the expansive territories of the Ottoman Empire. These tomes often include vivid case studies, providing granular detail that breathes both life and death into statistics. One might encounter heart-wrenching stories of untold hardships faced by rural and urban slaves, juxtaposed against the cold machinations of an economy that thrived on human misery.

Conferences and symposiums stand as hallowed grounds where scholars congregate, reviving ghosts of the past through fervent discourse and critical analysis. These gatherings transform academic symmetry into a dynamic, often contentious, exchange of ideas. The eloquence of keynote speeches, paper presentations, and panel discussions brings scholarly ink to life, creating an electrifying atmosphere where new hypotheses are born, challenged, and honed.

Such assemblages serve as crucibles for interdisciplinary collaboration, pulling in luminaries from history, sociology, economics, and beyond. The multidimensional platforms ignite dialogues that traverse the boundaries of individual disciplines, engendering a more cohesive understanding of the Caucasian slavery paradigm. Herein, historians deliver treatises on diplomatic dealings that sought to eradicate slavery, examining treaties and ransoms with surgical precision, while sociologists delve into the lasting societal impacts of this tragic epoch.

Invited speakers, often doyens in their respective fields, offer pivotal insights drawn from decades of painstaking research. Their addresses, while steeped in erudite aureole, are not without the pathos and gravitas befitting the subject matter. Explorations of public perception and media coverage during the time, alongside comparative analyses with the African slave trade, reveal the broader tapestry of societal collusion and silence that engulfed these atrocities.

Among the most revealing segments of these symposiums are the poster sessions and roundtable discussions, where burgeoning scholars present nascent ideas alongside seasoned experts. These interactions frequently expose gaps in existing research, prompting collaborative projects and funding initiatives aimed at uncovering further layers of historical truth. It is within these dynamic settings that the young aspirants of history often find their voices, emboldened by the communal pursuit of knowledge.

The arc of these gatherings frequently bends toward contemporary relevance, drawing parallels between historical injustices and current societal inequities. Panels dissect the modern-day implications, addressing issues of historical revisionism and the pernicious influence of educational gaps. Media representation is scrutinized, with experts advocating for more nuanced and comprehensive portrayals of slavery's multifaceted history in mainstream platforms.

Academic publications and conferences don't merely revisit the past; they compel forward motion toward reparative actions. Documented histories of memorials and reparative measures in specific regions serve as blueprints for current and future endeavors. Scholars passionately debate the efficacy of these initiatives, presenting success stories as well as cautionary tales, ensuring that modern efforts to address historical injustices are well-informed and impactful.

The ramifications of such scholarly activities are profound and far-reaching, fundamentally altering public narratives and educational curricula. Through fiery debates and meticulously researched publications, historians advocate for a heightened awareness that transcends academic echelons, seeping into public consciousness. Engaging with the past through rigorous scholarship fosters a moral imperative to grapple with and address the shadows it casts over the present.

Thus, the continuous churn of academic publications and the vibrant pulse of conferences serve an essential function—they demand that we confront the bleak corridors of our history, advocate for justice, and pave pathways toward collective healing. The inkwell runs deep, and the discourse, much like the haunting echoes of those lost to history, reverberates endlessly in the corridors of academic institutions and beyond.

Advocacy and Public Engagement

Historians stand not merely as chroniclers of times long gone but as architects of collective memory, the weavers of the intricate tapestry of human experience. In the realm of advocacy and public engagement, their role transforms from passive observers to active participants, wielding the power of knowledge to shape societal perceptions and memories. The relationship between history and public consciousness is both reciprocal and transformative. Advocates for historical truth carry the weighty responsibility of dismantling misconceptions and highlighting overlooked narratives, such as the plight of Caucasian slaves in the Ottoman Empire.

Central to this mission is the act of *telling*—telling the untold stories, giving voice to the silent, and shedding light on the shadows of history. Advocacy requires historians to step beyond the cloistered halls of academia and engage with the public sphere. Through lectures, public forums, and multimedia outreach, they breathe life into the dry bones of historical fact. The tales of those ensnared by the Barbary pirates, transported under the harshest conditions, and subjected to a life of relentless toil and terror need to be recounted with fervor and fidelity.

Academic publications alone cannot suffice. While peer-reviewed journals and scholarly books cast a meticulous eye on historical accuracy, they often reach only a limited audience. Advocacy entails broadening this reach, translating complex histories into accessible narratives. By participating in public debates, writing op-eds, and leveraging social media platforms, historians can bridge the chasm between scholarly research and public awareness. Their engagement fosters a public consciousness that values accuracy and empathy in the recounting of historical events.

Public history projects provide a tangible means to connect with communities. Museums, historical societies, and interactive exhibits serve as conduits for historical engagement. These platforms enable historians to create immersive experiences that resonate deeply. Imagine a museum exhibit that vividly reconstructs the plight of Caucasian slaves, showcasing their daily struggles, artifacts from their lives, and digital narratives that allow visitors to walk through the harrowing corridors of their existence. Such initiatives cultivate a space where history is not merely learned but felt.

Moreover, advocacy must endeavor to provoke critical thought and inspire action. Activism grounded in historical understanding can rally public support for reparative measures and memorials. Historians, in this context, act as guides, leading society towards confronting past injustices and fostering healing. Public lectures on platforms like TED Talks or community centers can galvanize support for recognizing the historical suffering of forgotten groups and advocating for their recognition in modern discourse.

The power of storytelling extends beyond the present, influencing future generations. Historians engaged in advocacy work with educators to integrate these crucial narratives into the fabric of educational curricula. Teaching the nuanced and often painful details of Caucasian slavery in schools can disrupt the prevailing historical narratives that frequently eclipse such stories. By influencing the curriculum, historians ensure that future generations inherit a balanced, inclusive, and accurate understanding of the past.

Furthermore, public engagement must wrestle with the complexities of historical memory. At times, societies prefer to forget uncomfortable truths, to gloss over the jagged edges of their past. Historians in their advocacy must challenge such selective amnesia. Engaging in public dialogues about historical revisionism, combating myths with meticulously researched truths, serves to protect the integrity of history. It is a defense against the erasure of the experiences of those who suffered unseen and unacknowledged.

Historians also harness the power of visual and digital media. Documentary films, historical dramas, and digital archives can reach vast audiences, evoking empathy and understanding through powerful visuals and narratives. By collaborating with filmmakers and digital archivists, historians ensure that the representations of Caucasian slavery are both accurate and compelling. These visual representations can often convey the depth of suffering and resilience in ways that words alone may struggle to capture.

Public engagement through art can serve as a poignant reminder of historical injustices. Statues, memorials, and public art installations dedicated to Caucasian slaves can serve as eternal witnesses to their profound suffering and resilience. These tangible markers in public spaces force society to confront its history head-on. They stand as silent yet powerful advocates for remembrance and reflection.

Historians must also engage with policymakers and lawmakers. In advocating for the recognition of historical injustices, they provide a wellspring of knowledge that can inform reparative legislation. Testimony based on historical facts can guide the creation of policies that address the remnants of past atrocities. In this way, historians become vital allies in the pursuit of justice, grounding modern actions in a thorough understanding of past wrongs.

In sum, advocacy and public engagement form the vital nexus through which historians influence societal understanding and remembrance of Caucasian slavery. Their role is proactive, demanding a delicate balance of empathy and rigor. By tirelessly advocating for the acknowledgment and understanding of these historical injustices, historians not only honor the memory of those who suffered but also guide society towards a more informed, just, and empathetic future. Through their efforts, the forgotten stories of Caucasian slaves gain voice, ensuring that their struggles and resilience are permanently etched into the collective human memory. This ceaseless endeavor shapes not only our understanding of the past but also the moral fabric of our present and future.

Chapter 12: Bridging Divides in Modern Society

Continuing our exploration of history's intricate web, we now traverse the chasms etched into the fabric of present-day society, drawing from the deep well of our collective past. In the annals of Caucasian slavery, there lies a stark reflection of today's fractured world. By examining the cruel tapestry of subjugation, where chains once shackled European souls within Ottoman confines, we unearth vital lessons echoing through time. These lessons, unencrusted by the patina of forgetfulness, whisper ardently of resilience and reconciliation. Correlating past and present, it becomes clear that the shadows of historical injustices linger, casting long reminders that unity arises not from ignoring the scars but from acknowledging them, learning, and striving to mend the divides. It is by this illumination from yesteryears that modern societies may navigate the labyrinthine realms of racial and cultural discord, forging a path toward a harmonious and inclusive future.

Lessons from History for Today's Issues

In the labyrinthine annals of history, where the shadows of Caucasian slavery unfurl, we glean invaluable insights pertinent to our modern milieu. The stark brutality endured by those enslaved in the Ottoman Empire impels us to scrutinize our current societal fissures with a discerning eye. Just as the chasm between master and slave was a product of dehumanization, today's divisions—whether they be racial, economic, or ideological—stem from similar roots of misunderstanding and prejudice. The scourge of history whispers to us, urging a conscientious remembrance and interpolation of those dark epochs into our collective consciousness. By understanding the mechanisms of alienation and subjugation that once orchestrated the lives of countless souls, we may forge a terrain of empathy and unity, thus bridging the divides that threaten to cleave our contemporary society asunder.

Relevant Case Studies and Comparisons often serve as the lens through which we unearth echoes from the past and extract lessons pivotal for contemporary society. In sifting through the annals of history, several case studies emerge as pertinent to the understanding of Caucasian slavery and its reverberations. These accounts, strewn with the specters of anguish and subjugation, provide us with a phantasmagoria of the complex interplay between human suffering, economic motivations, and societal hierarchies.

A foremost case worthy of mention is the capture of Icelanders during the Tyrkjaránið, or the Turkish Abductions of 1627. Barbary pirates, shrouded in the cloak of darkness, descended upon the shores of Iceland, mercilessly abducting around 400 individuals. This event not only thrust a hitherto isolated community into the grotesque mechanisms of slave trade but also laid bare the vulnerability of more peripheral European settlements. The severity of their plight was exacerbated by the interminable journeys they were forced to undertake, wedged beneath the prows of ships, their moans stifled by the ceaseless crashing of waves. This case implores us to draw grim parallels to modern instances of human trafficking, illustrating that despite temporal advancements, the malady of human exploitation endures.

Another striking comparison can be made with the fate of the Maltese slaves. Captured primarily during the raids of the 16th and 17th centuries, the Maltese found themselves plunged into a harrowing existence within the Ottoman realms. Their daily labor oscillated between tedious agricultural tasks and grueling stints in households laden with hierarchical disdain. Unlike the broad strokes of African slavery often peddled in mainstream discourse, these tales of Caucasian forced servitude splash diverse hues upon the canvas of historical injustices, compelling us to expand our collective memory.

The life of Thomas Pellow, an English boy snatched from the tranquil shores of Cornwall by Barbary corsairs in 1716, offers another vivid portrait. Pellow's subsequent twelve-year servitude under the tyrannical wrist of Sultan Moulay Ismail is meticulously chronicled in his memoir, providing a window into the ghastly conditions that defined slave life.

From enduring physical assaults to witnessing public executions, Pellow's narrative underscores the multifaceted nature of suffering inflicted upon Caucasian slaves, thereby serving as a poignant reminder of the various permutations of human cruelty.

The case study of the Knights of Saint John on the island of Malta provides further illumination. These knights not only engaged in counter-raids against Barbary pirates but also established a robust trade in enslaved captives themselves. The markets of Valletta thrived on the bartering of human lives; European captives found themselves sold alongside others, fate intertwining them with individuals from disparate geographies. This dual role of the knights reveals the contradictions and complexities within the mechanisms of slavery, emphasizing that the dichotomy of victim and oppressor is often blurred.

Delving further, the tale of Jan Janszoon, a Dutch privateer who metamorphosed into a Barbary corsair, showcases a convoluted narrative. After his capture, he embraced Islam and joined forces with the very pirates who had ensnared him, becoming a linchpin in subsequent slave raids on European coasts. Janszoon's story is not merely one of survival but illustrates the convoluted loyalties and transformations that coercive environments engender. It provides a riveting comparison with modern-day phenomena where victims sometimes assimilate within their oppressors' ranks out of sheer survival instinct.

The comparison of slavery in the Ottoman Empire with serfdom in Eastern Europe also warrants mention. While serfs were bound to the land and slaves to their owners, the fundamental essence of their plight shared chilling similarities. The term "slavery" may not have been uniformly brandished, yet the lives of serfs bore the brunt of destitution, enforced labor, and a near-absolute lack of mobility. By drawing these comparisons, we unravel the semantic layers that obscure our understanding of coerced labor across different historical contexts.

Notably, the plight of the Circassians holds another dark chapter within Caucasian slavery. Famed for their beauty, Circassian women were particularly coveted in harems, resulting in systematic raids on Circassian territories. This branding of human beings as commodities for aesthetic pleasure creates a ghastly prelude to contemporary issues of systemic objectification and exploitation. The Circassian saga serves as a morbid comparison to the ongoing global crises surrounding gender-based violence and human trafficking.

Even the Russian campaigns against the Ottoman Empire provide a paradoxical narrative. Russian soldiers, upon victory, often liberated enslaved Christians; however, they simultaneously perpetuated other forms of serfdom back home. This duality illuminates the irony within purported salvation tales, where rescue from one form of bondage might segue into another. Such dualities invite us to critique modern narratives that often ignore the complexities plastered behind simplified accounts of liberation and justice.

Through the looking glass of history, the paragon of the mutiny on the Spanish ship, "Concepción," emerges as a tale drenched in rebellion yet laced with the bittersweet taste of fleeting victories. Captured European slaves revolted against their Muslim captors, seizing control for a transient moment. Their act of defiance, though momentarily liberating, was ultimately quashed, symbolizing the ephemeral nature of rebellions within entrenched systems of oppression. This event mirrors the sporadic yet potent outbursts of resistance seen in various enslaved communities across different epochs, fostering a nuanced understanding of resilience in the face of subjugation.

The liberation of over 1,000 slaves in the 1816 bombardment of Algiers by the British fleet stands as a stark reminder of the international dimensions of the anti-slavery narrative. While European powers often participated in or tolerated slavery, they also, at times, spearheaded measures to curtail it. Such interventions underscore the complex and often contradictory roles that nations play within systems of exploitation. This historical episode draws parallels to present-day international human rights initiatives that oscillate between intervention and complicity.

Yet, not all reviews of Caucasian slavery should be steeped in abject gloom. Instances of manumission, where slaves managed to secure their freedom through various means, offer glimpses of hope. From industrious performances leading to the purchase of their own liberty to the philanthropy of benevolent masters, paths to emancipation, though rare, did exist. These narratives of eventual liberation find eerie reflections in contemporary stories of escape and reclamation of dignity among trafficked individuals worldwide.

In conclusion, the aforementioned case studies and comparisons elucidate the multifaceted nature of Caucasian slavery. By scrutinizing these accounts, we traverse beyond the monolithic portrayals of slavery, enriching our comprehension of its varied incarnations. Equally, these historical insights allow us to draw sobering connections to current issues of human exploitation, reminding us, the custodians of historical memory, that the specter of slavery, albeit transformed, continues to haunt the present.

Forging a Path Toward Unity

In the pages that precede this section, we dwelt deeply on the tendrils of history, unearthing the anguish and endurance of Caucasian slaves caught within the formidable grip of the Ottoman Empire. Now we turn our gaze forward, envisioning a terrain where the rifts etched by historical injustices are meticulously bridged. Yet, forging a path toward unity is not merely an evocative ideal; it is a colossal endeavor, fraught with intricacies and the mosaic complexities of human nature.

To weave together the torn fabric of society, we must first acknowledge the past. Unfurling the scrolls of history reveals not just the sufferings and sacrifices, but also the dormant wisdom inscribed within. Caucasian slaves, subjected to countless indignities, became unwitting historians of resilience. Their stories, laden with strife, manifest a profound testament to human endurance, and encapsulate lessons that transcend their epoch.

Consider the social schisms of our contemporary world. These divisions, often borne from ignorance and fanned by misinformation, echo the separations between master and slave, oppressor and oppressed. The pressing need for unified societal fabric echoes across ages. We, the inheritors of such a fractured history, look upon the past not as a bygone era, but as a mirror reflecting the discord we strive to overcome today.

Let us contemplate the construction of unity through the lens of shared suffering. The agony of the Caucasian slaves, recorded in annals draped in sorrow, speaks with a universal tone of affliction. It whispers of unity forged in the crucible of collective torment. However, this unity is not birthed from the mere acknowledgment of shared pain, but from the committed endeavor to right the chronic wrongs that continue to ripple through the present.

To delineate a tangible pathway to unity, we embark on the earnest endeavor of education. Enlightening the masses about seminal historical injustices becomes paramount. The stories of Caucasian slaves must be inked into curricula, discussed in academic forums, and magnified by the luminosity of media. Erasure or ignorance of such history creates voids where prejudice festers.

Furthermore, unity demands empathy, a profound and empathetic understanding that allows individuals to step into the harrowing shoes of those long gone and those suffering in the present. It requires the dismantling of apathy and the cultivation of an empathic gaze towards one another. As we learn of the Caucasian slaves who toiled incessantly, we recognize their unending hope for liberation; a hope that reverberates across generations. Such an empathetic approach paves the way for a society that values every individual's liberty and dignity.

The role of dialogue cannot be overstated in this quest. Conversations, open and unbridled, must ensue between communities. The reminiscent echoes of eluded freedom and the valiant fights of these slaves can act as catalysts for discussions about modern bonds of discrimination and servitude, thus fostering understanding and a concerted fight against contemporary injustices. In these dialogues, we discover kindred spirits across divides, drawing ever closer to unity.

Examining the economic ramifications of slavery also elucidates pathways toward unity. Caucasian slaves contributed significantly to the Ottoman Empire's economy, underpinning societal structures with their labor. These contributions are often understated, lost amidst broader historical narratives. Acknowledging and compensating for these contributions through reparative justice can mend financial disparities that linger from older systems of oppression. Unity, thus, isn't an abstract ideal but finds root in tangible and equitable measures.

The metaphorical weight of chains can only be lifted through societal acknowledgement and repentance. Public monuments, museums, and memorials serve not just as reminders of past injustices but also as beacons of our commitment to rectify historical wrongs. By investing in such endeavors, society bridges the abyss between the specters of history and the aspirations of a just future.

Yet unity demands more than mere contrition; it calls for active and deliberate inclusion. As Caucasian slaves were shackled by chains literal and figurative, modern society witnesses many still bound by unemployment, inequality, and invisibility. Policies and practices that emphasize diversity and equal opportunity can transform this vision into reality. Historical awareness underscores that inclusivity is an irrevocable right, not a selective privilege.

Unity is further cemented through historical narratives that encapsulate both the broad strokes and nuanced details of our collective past. Historians must wield their quills not only to recount but to advocate, to turn fading memories into compelling calls for unity. The stories of Caucasian slaves, meticulously documented, provide a blueprint for understanding the relentless human spirit and fostering mutual respect.

Furthermore, unity rests on the scaffold of justice. Legislative reforms, grounded in historical contexts, create frameworks where such injustices do not recur. By examining past statutes that facilitated slavery and contrasting them with modern laws, historians can advocate for robust legal frameworks to protect liberties.

Thus, our journey towards unity is not a linear path but a weaving tapestry, rich with the stories of those who suffered and struggled, yet dreamt of freedom. As historians, it is our endeavor to highlight these struggles, ensuring that Caucasian slaves are remembered not as voiceless victims but as beacons guiding us towards a unified and equitable society.

Conclusion

In delving into the obscure and oft-ignored history of Caucasian slavery, we illuminate a facet of human suffering that has long lurked in the shadows of collective memory. The agony and tribulation endured by these forgotten souls serve as a stark reminder of the depths to which humanity can descend. As historians, it is our solemn duty to unearth the veiled corners of history, to ensure the stories buried beneath centuries of dust and denial see the light once more. The oubliette of our past must not detain the testimony of the voiceless, for the revelation of their plight enriches our understanding and fosters a more comprehensive view of human bondage.

The grim odyssey of the Caucasian slaves reminds us that history's pages are inked with the pain of myriad sufferings. The Barbary pirates, with their sinister raids and brutal transport conditions, hauled souls into a life of ceaseless toil and torment. These chains not only fettered the flesh but maimed the spirit. Society's indifference then, mirrored now in the widespread apathy towards certain contemporary issues, indicates a foreboding cycle of ignorance that threatens to repeat itself.

The exploitation that stitched the Ottoman Empire's wealth and societal structure together left scars visible and invisible, both on individuals and the collective psyche. Their anguish, laboring in fields, households, and through inhumane punishments, is not merely a cautionary tale but a testament to resilience amid despair. Yet, these narratives have been eclipsed by the more frequently studied atrocities of other forms of slavery, particularly the transatlantic slave trade. It is an academic and moral imperative to open our canvas to these silenced voices.

Severing the past might seem a salve for the guilt of history, but without recognition and understanding, it festers, breeding grounds for repeated injustices. The perceived hierarchies and social strata imposed upon them, their roles within Ottoman society — urban elites versus rural laborers — paint a portrait of a world that seems simultaneously distant and disconcertingly familiar. They resisted, a testament not to the triumph of tyranny but to the indomitable human spirit, a quiet, persistent heartbeat against the cacophony of oppression. Their resistance, subtle or overt, is the flame that flickers defiantly against the encroaching darkness.

As we examine the diplomatic wranglings and public perceptions of the time, we must consider if our ancestors' blind spots have not become our own. Are we not engaged in an eternal struggle to confront and rectify the systemic injustices lingering from eras gone by? Treaties and ransoms, social narratives, and cultural interpretations oscillated between condemnation and complicity, shaping a public discourse that often muddied the waters of moral clarity.

The enduring legacy of Caucasian slavery stretches its tendrils into the very fabric of modern Europe and the remnants of the Ottoman realm. The genetic imprints and cultural syncretism left in their wake evoke both pride and poignance. It is a reminder that our identities are a mosaic crafted from myriad sources of light and shadow. The modern historical narratives we construct must, therefore, embrace these complexities, lest we fall into the simplicity of selective remembrance.

In comparing the fates of Caucasian slaves to their African counterparts, we discern both commonalities and stark divergences. The unique roles they fulfilled within the Ottoman Empire, juxtaposed with statistical data, lay bare the multifaceted nature of slavery itself, transcending reductive dichotomies. Such comparisons challenge us to eschew simplistic binaries, urging instead for a more nuanced interpretation of human history's convulsions.

As contemporary historians, our discourse should not shy away from these unpleasant truths. Modern ignorance and apathy towards the dark chapters of our past could doom us to repeat these mistakes, a transgression historians such as ourselves must hinder. An unerring dedication to filling educational gaps, accurately representing media, and confronting historical revisionism calls upon us to wield our scholarship as a shield against the erosion of truth.

Addressing historical injustices isn't merely an exercise in acknowledgment but rather a journey toward reparation and reconciliation. Memorials, reparative measures, and success stories from other contexts provide frameworks for healing and moving forward. These efforts bind the wounds of history, allowing societies to mend their fractures with informed, compassionate action.

The historian's role, far from being a passive observer, is one of active engagement. Investigating, advocating, and disseminating our findings through academic and public channels invigorates the scholarly endeavor. Through publications, conferences, and compelling advocacy, we shape public memory and policy, contributing inexorably to a more just future.

In drawing the curtain on this exploration, we must reflect upon how the lessons etched in the annals of Caucasian slavery can bridge modern divides. Historical case studies and comparative analyses provide us with cautionary tales and sources of inspiration, guiding us toward a path of unity in an increasingly fragmented world. The past does not merely haunt us; it offers a compass by which we might navigate the troubled waters of the present. It is incumbent upon us, the bearers of historical wisdom, to cast light where shadows dwell and to ever strive toward forging a collective memory that dignifies all human experience.

Appendix A: Appendix

In this compendium of sorrow and resilience, we find an enduring testament to the shadows that history often casts upon the present. The appendix, a vessel of ancillary insights and meticulous references, seeks to anchor the narrative threads woven throughout this tome. Herein lies a collection of supplemental materials that extend beyond the mere recounting of events, to encapsulate the full breadth of the Caucasian slave experience under Ottoman rule.

The materials amassed include detailed charts mapping the proliferation of the slave trade, lists of primary source documents that bear witness to the trials endured, and an index of significant figures whose lives were irrevocably altered by the chains of bondage. Such artifacts not only corroborate the tales expounded within the chapters but also offer a profound glimpse into the interwoven fates of captors and captives alike.

To the discerning historian, these additional documents provide the sinews that bind the skeletal framework of our dialogue. They are intended to furnish the ardent scholar with the means to traverse the epochs with confidence and clarity. Not insubstantial in their gravity, these appendices attest to the meticulousness required to confront history's more harrowing tableaux.

Reference Materials

- **Primary Source Documents:** Translated manuscripts, decrees, and letters exemplifying the discourse of the era.
- **Economic Data:** Tabulated records of slave market revenues, price fluctuations, and fiscal reports from key locales within the Ottoman dominion.
- **Diaries and Personal Narratives:** Firsthand accounts from those ensnared in the web of slavery, lending humanity to historical abstractions.

Tables and Charts

- **Origins and Destinations:** Maps delineating the routes carved by Barbary corsairs, juxtaposed with statistical tables depicting captured demographics.
- **Social Stratification:** Schematics drawing contrasts between slave hierarchies in urban and rural environs.
- **Comparison Metrics:** Analytical charts comparing the lived experiences of Caucasian slaves with those subjected to other forms of servitude, offering a visual representation of disparities and commonalities.

Notable Figures

- **Captives of Prominence:** Biographical sketches of slaves who achieved notable status or whose plights garnered contemporary attention.
- **Key Abolitionists:** Profiles of the diplomats, activists, and scholars who labored tirelessly to dismantle the institution of slavery within the Ottoman realm.
- **Witnesses and Chroniclers:** Individuals whose records and testimonies provide critical insights into the complexities of Ottoman slavery.

In perusing the appendix, one engages not merely with the residual echoes of the past but assumes a role in preserving the integrity and completeness of the historical record. Let these documents, lists, and figures serve as a beacon for those who seek to fathom the unfathomable depths of Caucasian enslavement, ensuring that the suffering and fortitude of those souls are neither forgotten nor misrepresented.